Scotlands, 1 1994

Typeset in Berkeley Old Style by
ROM-Data Limited, Falmouth, Cornwall
and printed and bound in Great Britain
by Page Bros Limited, Norwich, Norfolk

ISSN 1350–7508

Scotlands is supported by the St Andrews Scottish Studies Institute, University
of St Andrews, and the Scottish Studies Association, University of Waikato

Introduction

Whether Scotland will emerge from *Scotlands* as a whole entity is a major question. We launch this interdisciplinary magazine at a time when the idea of single cultural concepts is under strain. The subject of this first issue, the canons of Scottish culture, is full of precisely this tension. For three centuries the Scots have striven to maintain and assert a national culture, and now the whole notion of centralised canons is thrown in doubt. The structures of coherence and hegemony devised by the English-speaking communities in Britain and North America, against which Scottish culture has in the past measured itself, are now fiercely questioned from within. Ironically, those structures, and the model upon which they are based, owe much to Scottish thinkers; Hume's history, Smith's economics, Frazer's anthropology, Murray's etymology and much else of Scottish intellectual provenance, contributed mightily to the so-called imperialist culture against which post-modernism wishes to rebel. Not that the Scots simply meant to build universal norms. Their interest in what was essential to the foundation of a national culture in Britain and America was also a search for guidelines for more local use; if Scotland remained a nation after its crown and parliament went to London, then the soul of a nation was a more abstruse thing than a monarch and a legislature. But whatever it was it seemed it must be one thing, variegated, complex, richly diverse, perhaps, but held together by some power of convergence, or centred on some essential national *geist*. No group of human beings could claim nationhood without, it seemed, the possession of centralised canons of language, literature, history, art, politics and much else, and the task of a would-be nation's intelligentsia was to nurture the canonical.

Scotland was close to the leaders of this movement. The image of Scotland came together very quickly at the end of the eighteenth century and was soon after fixed and broadcast to the world almost single-handedly by Sir Walter Scott. Wherever his novels went in Europe they catalysed the foundation of national canons of literature and history, which sparked in turn the struggles for unification and self-determination of a dozen nations. Ironically again, while these asserted their independence, Scotland was left with a form of nationhood that lacked specific political expression, despite increasingly vigorous efforts, especially in the twentieth century, to make the break-through from cultural to political nationalism which seemed to have been the genesis of most of the smaller (and some of the larger) nations of Europe. Frustratingly, what the Scots had pioneered and what seemed to work for other peoples refused to take place in Scotland itself.

Now, as the twentieth century closes, commentators on culture announce the obsolescence of the model Scotland has for so long stubbornly struggled to follow. The intellectual leaders of the dominating national cultures of the western world, France, England and the United States of America, proclaim the death of the Enlightenment ideals of the general will, state-directed art and education, and the integrated self. The attacks on literary canons as exclusivist, disguised assertions of power, on national history as propaganda for traditional ruling classes and on the whole concept of state-supported culture as a device for ignoring difference and imposing order all strike at the conventional programme for national unity. The political and intellectual consequences of these revolts against uniformity and in favour of diversity have yet to be worked out, but it is certain that the old concept of a community of people united by language, culture, geography and political convention will be radically revised.

Where this leaves the traditional attitudes to Scotland and Scottish culture is likewise unresolved, but it may be that just because Scotland's nationhood has been problematic for two hundred years (at least) it is easier to ask the right questions in Scotland's case than in many others. If Scotland did not become a nineteenth-century nation because its internal differences could not be reconciled, because its external links were too strong to be ignored, because its history was resistant to resolution, because its literature refused to be contained, and because its art contended with the parochial and its science and scholarship were not content with less than international concerns, then perhaps Scotland's is a nationalism which could be open to the post-modern ideals of dialogue, diversity and decentralisation. It may be that Scotland is ready for the reshaping of its idea of itself. Besides, it is the case that Scottish self-awareness, and Scottish awareness of the world beyond, and awareness of Scotland in the world beyond, have burgeoned in the last quarter of this century. In Germany, in France, in Canada, in the United States, in New Zealand and in many places between, Scottish studies have become a focus for university institutes and academic journals and societies, matching a similar growth in Scottish studies within Scotland. As the articles in this first issue of *Scotlands* show, Scottish scholars, and scholars of Scotland, are now at the point of having much to say about their Scotlands, and much of what they say revises those traditional ideas which are at the centre of modern intellectual debate. Out of this ferment of ideas will emerge a new image of Scotland, a pluralistic, syncretic Scotland, an international Scotland. We hope that the place to discuss this emergence is a journal dedicated to the concept of a pluralist nation, and a journal with a title that declares this – *Scotlands*.

Future Issues

Scotlands is an interdisciplinary and international magazine about Scotland, hence the plurality of its title. In its pages will be reflected the views of historians, literary critics, social scientists, art historians, musicians and any other profession which has something to say about Scotland, past, present and future. By bringing together commentators from as wide a range of disciplines as possible, and from outside as well as inside Scotland itself, we hope to display a Scotland with more facets than any other single journal presents. We also hope that the opportunity to publish particular views in one forum will inspire comparisons and connections between ideas and approaches which otherwise might be missed. The chance will be there not only for readers to see links between items in *Scotlands* but also for contributors to build bridges out from their own specialisms, to open up their own debates to speakers from other dialogues and to acknowledge that their Scotland is not the only one. This is intellectually risky. Pretentiousness and wishful thinking stalk the borders between subject disciplines. But where subject-specific journals must play safe and keep their material firmly centred, *Scotlands* will encourage speculation and the transgression of boundaries. We think there is a place for scholars, critics, experts and all those involved in Scottish studies and Scottish culture to raise their heads from what their disciplines impose as norms and ask bigger questions and suggest bigger answers than any one discipline can claim to do. We intend that *Scotlands* should be that place.

A principal cause of the revision of the concept of the nation state has been the rise of feminism. Women's consciousness of their exclusion from the language, the iconography and the power structures of the traditional nation state and its cultural self-projections has driven the assault on the monolithic assumptions upon which that state is built. In the process the form and content of cultural expression have been searchingly criticised for those glib assertions of male preference which disguise themselves as universal truths. The claims made by women for representation and recognition for themselves have overturned the masculine consensus, and allowed other groups to demand a voice, too. In the second issue of *Scotlands* we will concentrate on the effect of feminism on Scottish studies in an edition devoted to gender issues. In our third issue we will acknowledge the international dimension of the Scottish nation by focussing on the colonial experience, bringing forward those Scotlands which have been created around the world. For Scotland has long since outgrown the top half of the north-west European archipelago where it happens to lie. It is a country of the mind as big and diverse as any continent, and *Scotlands* is its atlas. ❧

COLIN KIDD

The canon of patriotic landmarks in Scottish history

Scotland is an historic nation, and after almost three centuries of incorporation within the British state its people still retain a sense of a national identity more comprehensive than mere regionalism. Nevertheless, this historic nationhood lacks a convincing vehicle of historical expression. Whereas over the last two centuries many of the historic and recreated nations of Europe promoted historiographical traditions emphasising national self-determination as the basis of freedom,[1] in modern Scotland there has been no widely acceptable body of patriotic history which challenges the incorporation of the Scots nation within the British state as a restriction of Scottish liberties. Criticism of English oppression is safely contained within the distant medieval era, in a national crisis which was resolved in favour of continued independence. The medieval War of Independence, the deeds of Wallace and Bruce and the Declaration of Arbroath remain the brightest lodestars of Scottish patriotic history, yet they do very little to illuminate Scotland's present predicament. Nor do popular memories of the tragic fate of Mary, Queen of Scots, or the Jacobite rebellions constitute a compelling national *mythistoire*. The Scottish past as an ideological resource is virtually bankrupt. Why is the canon of Scottish patriotic cynosures so impoverished? And does the recent renaissance in Scottish historical writing hold out the prospect of a more confident vision of Scotland's past?

   The impoverishment of Scottish patriotic history began only in the eighteenth century when the critical scholarship of Father Thomas Innes (1662-1744), and the sociological and philosophical perspectives of the Scottish Enlightenment, undermined the intellectual foundations of the powerful historical mythology which had enthralled the late medieval and early modern political nation. Half a century following the Scottish War of Independence, a creative mythmaker, the chronicler John of Fordun (c.1320–

c.1384), constructed a bold and influential interpretation of the course of Scottish history which was to dominate the nation's political culture until the mid eighteenth century. The evolution and elaboration of Fordun's seminal vision embrace the progression of Scottish historical writing from the straightforward monastic chronicle via the polished moralism of humanist narrative to the polemical historical tracts typical of the constitutional debates of the seventeenth and early eighteenth centuries. Yet the Fordunian myth withered under the rigorous standards of enlightened historiography. The prominent features of Fordunian history which had dominated the landscape of patriotic expression and political debate for four centuries were obliterated. A majority of the canonical shibboleths were discredited, and ideological coherence was lost. This collapse and fragmentation of the late medieval canon of patriotic cynosures was the prelude to the pitiful version of the nation's history in popular currency today.

The cultural leaders of fourteenth-century Scotland could not afford the luxury of detachment enjoyed by the polished North British university-men of the Enlightenment. Fordun's invention was a product of ideological necessity. The success of Fordun's chronicle derived from its refutation of the story of the origins of Britain found in the chronicle of Geoffrey of Monmouth (d.1155), used by the Plantagenet kings of England as the basis of their claims to be overlords of Scotland. Fordun constructed a counter-history of the origins of the Scottish kingdom. He extended the traditional account of the arrival of the Scots in the West Highlands and the creation of the Dalriadic monarchy under King Fergus MacErch in the Dark Ages back to the fourth century B.C. and a supposed ancestor, Fergus MacFerquhard, posthumously created King of Scotland. This mythical timeframe allowed Scots to claim priority of settlement in Britain, and to affirm the legitimacy of their independent and sovereign possession of Scottish territory. In this way Scots challenged the applicability, and indeed veracity, of Geoffrey of Monmouth's account of the founding of Britain: that the first king, Brutus, bequeathed, by a sort of gavelkind, England and the suzerainty of the whole of Britain, to his eldest son Locrinus, and the subordinate crowns of Scotland and Wales to his younger sons Albanacht and Camber.[2]

Although some of the constituent parts of the patriotic canon had been present in earlier chronicles, had featured in the genealogies of the Scottish royal line recited by sennachies at coronations, and had been deployed in the heat of the ideological struggle with England in the early fourteenth century, most notably in the Barons' Letter to the Pope, the Declaration of Arbroath, it was Fordun in his chronicle who cast the mould of Scotland's usable past. Fordun discarded some existing elements of Scottish patriotism, such as the legend of the Scythian origins of the Scots, and constructed a new and lengthened chronology for the Scots kingdom. At first these innovations were contradicted by patriotic historians and mythographers such as Andrew of Wyntoun (c.1355–1422) and John Barbour (?1320–95) who adhered to some of the pre-Fordunian cynosures. However, Walter Bower (c.1385–1449) continued and strengthened the work of Fordun, and, in time, Fordun's systematic overhaul of Scottish history came to be the near-exclusive determinant of patriotic historiography, providing the raw material upon which later generations of Scottish historians might elaborate.[3]

For almost the next four centuries, Scots continued to use the history of their formation as a political community under the rule of Fergus MacFerquhard to counter English pretensions to an imperial suzerainty over Scotland. This argument for the high antiquity of the Scottish kingdom was of especial importance after 1603, when it defended Scots from English claims to superiority within the composite monarchy of the Union of the Crowns. In the initial decades following the Union of 1707 it still remained necessary to use this origin myth to stifle any English suggestions that incorporating union was not a treaty between two fully sovereign states, but merely masked the reabsorption by the imperial crown of England of a rebellious subordinate monarchy. The myth of Fergusian antiquity was reinforced by other elements in the patriotic canon. Romano-Caledonian archaeology frustrated the English claim that the sovereignty of Roman Britannia, having devolved on the kings of the Britons, and then to their Saxon and Norman successors, entailed an empire over the whole island of Britain: Hadrian's Wall and the Antonine Wall seemed to prove that very little of Scotland had ever been incorporated within the Roman Empire. The treaty supposedly made between the Scottish king, Achaius, and the Emperor Charlemagne was cited as evidence of an independent Scottish foreign policy. Since it was contrary to the feudal law for a vassal to make such alliances, Achaius was clearly unaware of his subordination to the English crown. Moreover, Scots went further than merely affirming their independence: they also boasted that while the peoples of south Britain had been invaded successfully by waves of Romans, Saxons, Danes and Normans, the Scots, by their superior martial valour, had preserved their freedom intact from all comers.[4]

Fordun's most influential successors were the humanist historians Hector Boece (c.1465–1536) and George Buchanan (1506–82), who imposed on the skeleton of Fordun's history schemes of moral and political *exempla*. Boece and Buchanan used the reigns of Scottish kings and the vicissitudes of the nation's past to address such topics as good governance, civic virtue and tyranny. This humanist gloss, particularly in Buchanan's history of Scotland, *Rerum Scoticarum Historia*, (1582) and political treatise, *De Iure Regni Apud Scotos* (1579), added a new polemical dimension to the Fordunian canon. The foundation of the monarchy by Fergus MacFerquhard in 330 B.C. now achieved ancient constitutional status: a crucial site of prescriptive legitimacy at the birth of the kingdom which ordained the proper domestic relations of the Scottish crown and political nation. The same ancient terrain on which Scots patriots from Fordun onwards had done battle with the propagandists of an English pan-Britannic empire became a fount of domestic constitutional legitimacy. In the sixteenth and seventeenth centuries, royalist proponents of absolute monarchy and their opponents, monarchomach resistance theorists, struggled to appropriate this central cynosure of Scottish patriotism. Later, the ideological successors of those traditions, Jacobite and Whig respectively, continued the same ancient constitutional debate into the first half of the eighteenth century.[5]

The canon of early modern Scotland's historical politics comprised a series of precedents which demonstrated the operation of the principles of the ancient constitution in the national past. The central issue was whether Fergus MacFerquhard at the foundation of the Scottish monarchy had become king by hereditary right in the line of Irish Scotic kings; or had, by his own exertions, made himself king, forging the Scots settlers in the West Highlands into a political community; or had been elected king either by the people as a whole or by the phylarchs, or clan leaders, of the Scottish tribes. These varying interpretations offered different solutions to the vexed question of the legitimate form of Scotland's government: whether the monarchy was absolute, or at least indefeasibly hereditary; or elective, with monarchs accountable to nobles or people. Other events in the history of the Scottish kingdom were identified with the operation of the principles of the ancient constitution. Of central importance in the canon of historical precedents was the law of Kenneth II (or III according to the Fergusian style of numbering) transforming Scotland into a hereditary monarchy. Monarchomachs and Whigs interpreted this as the subversion of the ancient elective constitution, royalists and Jacobites as the rectification of creeping abuses which had perverted the original hereditary law of the succession of 330 B.C. Other controversies prominent in the canon of historical politics included such questions as whether the importation of feudal tenures into Scotland had been by royal fiat or consent, and whether Robert Bruce had become king by hereditary right or by election.[6]

There was also an ecclesiastical dimension to Scotland's usable past. Fordun located the conversion of the Scots to Christianity in 203 during the pontificate of Victor I, and Boece went on to identify this era with the reign of King Donald. In time this myth was elaborated further, first, in the late sixteenth century, as a non-Petrine mission to Scotland which affirmed the freedom of Reformed Scotland from the claims of Rome, and later by both rival presbyterian and episcopalian historians who gave different twists to this ancient Scottish ecclesiastical constitution. The presbyterians argued that the early church in Scotland had been governed by colleges of proto-presbyterian monks called Culdees, who had not been subordinated to episcopal authority. Episcopalians used the myth of the ancient conversion of Scotland to argue that the Church of Scotland was in its original constitution an independent, or autocephalous, national church governed by bishops but owing no allegiance either to Rome or to the metropolitan claims of Canterbury. In this way the myth of the ancient origins of the Church of Scotland functioned as a direct ecclesiastical parallel to the myth of Fergus MacFerquhard in defining the state.[7]

With the rage of partisanship in church and state which followed the Revolution of 1689, the old Fordunian canon, albeit with judicious trimming, amendment and adornment over the years, still supplied Scotland's ideological needs in a variety of spheres. However, in 1729 the Jacobite antiquarian Father Innes undermined the 'factual' basis of Scottish antiquity, which had comprised the most usable material of the Fordunian canon. Innes tried to replace the ancient constitution of Fergus MacFerquhard with an ancient hereditary Pictish monarchy. Although these Pictish seeds failed to germinate, Innes had succeeded in felling the supporting trunk of the traditional canon.[8]

The historians of the Scottish Enlightenment completed the destruction of the established canon of Scottish historiography. The sociological historians of the Scottish Enlightenment, who included David Hume (1711–76), William Robertson (1721–93), Adam Smith (1723–90), Henry Home, Lord Kames (1696–1782), Adam Ferguson (1723–1816) and John Millar (1735–1801), deconstructed the criteria upon which the existing framework of Scottish history had been built. They attacked the anachronisms inherent in ancient constitutionalist argument, and challenged some of the central ideas of traditional Scottish Whiggism, such as the overriding importance of limitations on monarchy as a measure of liberty. Instead, this new wave of historical sociologists argued that civil liberty, or the freedom and security of people and property, were more important than Scotland's much vaunted history of limited monarchy. Not only was the currency of Scotland's patriotic historical politics declared counterfeit, but, by the standards of the new sociological history of liberty constructed in the Scottish Enlightenment, Scotland's independent past was deemed an almost unmitigated disaster. The historical sociologists interpreted the rise of modern civil liberty in terms of the subtle interaction of institutions, laws, economic practices, social structures, beliefs and manners. As far as the Scottish Enlightenment was concerned, Scotland had failed on all these fronts. Her unicameral parliament, its deliberations dominated by Scotland's feudal magnate caste, and its agenda until 1690 controlled by the Lords of the Articles, had not protected the liberties of the Scottish people. Scots law had been a tool of the feudal baronage, whose heritable jurisdictions were not abolished until 1747.

Scottish economic history was a story of agrarian backwardness only relieved by a post-Union drive for improvement. The Lowlands had stagnated under a very slowly defeudalising social structure; in the Highlands such was the dominance of arbitrary chiefs, unchecked by written leases, that civil society could not properly be said to exist. Early modern presbyterianism came under assault as a dangerous form of fanaticism which had retarded the progress of Scottish civil society by disrupting the social order required for economic development. The customs of many groups in Scottish society, including feudal superiors, the holders of strict entails, traditional presbyterians, and most Highlanders, were viewed as inimical to the evolution of civil liberty in Scotland. The rise of personal liberty in mid eighteenth-century Scotland was attributed to the accident of the incorporating Union of 1707, in effect to a contingency whereby Scotland had been able to cast off most of her backward and oppressive institutions, more following in the legislative bonfire which followed the Jacobite rebellion of 1745. A modern Whiggism arose which was anti-feudalist, anglicised and critical of most of the traditional patriotic formulations of Scottish history. As a result of the devastation caused by the Scottish Enlightenment, those features of the standard canon of historical events which had survived the scholarly assault of Innes were now cut loose from their former moorings – a discredited political philosophy – and cast adrift on a sea of historical meaninglessness.[9]

This process was exacerbated by the taming of Jacobitism. Once it ceased to be a political threat, a neo-Jacobite escapist history emerged which offered no ideological challenge to the entrenched values of Whiggism, but which muddied the ideological significance of the remnants of Scottish patriotic historiography. A central figure in this process was Sir Walter Scott (1771–1832), whose association with romantic neo-Jacobitism was qualified by his adherence to the modern Whig tenets of the Scottish Enlightenment. Scott's achievement as national mythmaker did not consist in creating an assertive Scots nationalist historiography, but in celebrating the consolidation of a previously divided Scottish people into a common body. The *Waverley Novels* record the disasters of Scottish history – the conflicts of Highlander and Lowlander, Covenanter and episcopalian, Whig and Jacobite – and the eventual triumph of civility over division in the second half of the eighteenth century. Scott purveyed a nationalist interpretation of the Scottish past only insofar as he advanced anti-sectarian and anti-sectional messages. He welcomed the rise of a peaceful civil society in Scotland, and a genuinely national moral community which transcended old divisions. In the historical tradition of Fordun and Buchanan the different ethnic components of the Scottish kingdom, such as the Picts, Galloway Britons, Saxons, Normans, Bretons and Flemings, had been subordinated to the story of the Scots of Dalriada. By contrast, Scott's vision was pluralist. It encompassed the Borders, the

Highlands, the cities of Glasgow and Edinburgh, the Orkneys and the small burghs of the east coast. As a child of the Enlightenment, Scott accepted the view that before 1707 Scotland had been an oppressed and backward feudal kingdom. Although Scott succeeded heroically in reconciling the contradictions generated by Scotland's historic intestine broils, he was unable to mend the torn garment of her formerly vigorous and meaningful national past. Indeed, Scott was able to succeed in the former task largely because he transmuted the ideologies fuelling Scotland's internal hatreds into historical novels which captured the deeply-held beliefs of all parties. In his own historical politics Scott fused sentimental Jacobitism with a mild Whiggism; in such novels as *Old Mortality* and *Rob Roy* he celebrated the Revolution of 1689 and the Union of 1707, while engaging the reader's sympathy for the causes of Cavalier and Jacobite. By applying a sentimental Jacobite gloss to a basic Whig constitutionalism, Scott turned the Scottish past into an ideologically neutral pageant – suitable material for historical romance, but incapable of supporting a romantic nationalist historiography of either an authoritarian or liberal hue. In the words of Nicholas Phillipson, he transformed Scottish nationalism into 'an ideology of noisy inaction'. Yet Scott's failure is also his triumph, a creative response to his awareness, painful for someone with such a passionate interest in Scottish history, that civil peace and social harmony depended upon defusing the nation's past.[10]

Scott was a crucial catalyst in the process which, in the Victorian era, culminated in what the late Marinell Ash has described as 'the strange death of Scottish history'.[11] Nineteenth-century Scottish patriotism was bequeathed a bowdlerised historical canon: a very loose collection of incidents without a plot or a unifying thread of constitutional development. Moreover, Scotland's historical totems were ideologically muddled. John Knox, Mary, Queen of Scots, the Covenanters and the band of Scottish Jacobite heroes were juxtaposed without any regard to their status as political symbols within different partisan traditions in Scottish political and ecclesiastical history. Loss of partisan significance impaired their function as patriotic exemplars: this set of neutered icons suggested no particular definition of Scottish nationhood. They became aimless characters in a hybrid surrealist-romantic drama which, though swashbuckling, leads nowhere. Thus was born, after a long gestation from the Scottish Enlightenment to the Victorian era, the debased canon of Scottish history which still dominates the national memory.

Although the institutional history of Scotland had been discredited, the history of personal achievement remained a vital part of Scottish patriotism. From the seventeenth century, cultural historiography had vigorously championed national pride. The Roman Catholic émigré and patriotic hagiographer, Thomas Dempster (1579?–1625), appropriated saints from Ireland by playing on the confused medieval identity of Scotia in his *Historia ecclesiastica gentis Scotorum* (Bologna, 1627); Thomas Urquhart of Cromarty (1611–60) launched the cult of the Admirable Crichton (c.1560–85); Scottish success in neo-Latin literature was glorified by such writers as Dr George Mackenzie (1669–1725), who also followed Dempster in adding a few Irish saints and scholars to the canon of Scottish cultural heroes. Scottish successes in the martial arts formed the subject of laudatory histories, such as Patrick Abercromby's *The Martial Achievements of the Scots Nation* (2 vols., 1711–15). Cultural patriotism crossed partisan boundaries; even royalists and Jacobites who anathematised Buchanan's politics of resistance and king-killing championed the work of Scotland's greatest neo-Latin prose stylist. Although the eighteenth century witnessed the destruction of Scotland's conventional patriotic history, pride in the humanist spheres of arms and letters continued.[12]

The historians of the Scottish Enlightenment, while they undermined Scottish patriotic institutional historiography, not only acknowledged a genuine history of Scottish cultural successes, but were themselves incorporated into the canon of intellectual achievement. Hume was struck by the contrast between the standing of eighteenth-century Scotland in the world of learning, and the poverty of her recent historical experience as a nation:

> Is it not strange that, at a time when we have lost our princes, our parliaments, our independent government, even the presence of our chief nobility, are unhappy in our accent and pronunciation, speak a very corrupt dialect of the tongue which we make use of; is it not strange, I say, that in these circumstances, we should really be the people most distinguished for literature in Europe?

As if answering Hume's conundrum, John Millar integrated a patriotic celebration of Scottish intellectual achievements within the framework of his negative account of Scotland's economic and institutional underdevelopment. He attributed intellectual successes such as the Scottish Enlightenment to early modern Scotland's economic backwardness, among other factors. The popular ferment which attended the Scottish Reformation had created an enthusiasm among the 'common mass of the people' for 'the various points of theological controversy'; and as they became 'conversant in many abstract disquisitions' connected with religion, developed a more general intellectual 'curiosity'. The Union of the Crowns destroyed Scottish court culture and the status of the Scots tongue, forcing Scottish writers to turn to philosophical topics. This had created a culture of knowledge rather than expression. Yet Millar also believed that the backwardness of the Scottish economy had allowed this culture to develop. Scotland's remaining 'for a long time in that simple state of society which precedes the minute division of labour among the different kind of artificers', meant that, instead of becoming 'mere mechanical drudges' like the population of England, Scots had retained a relish for fashionable learning.[13]

In the nineteenth century a new cast of missionaries, empire-builders, explorers, inventors and scientists broadened the national pantheon and consolidated a vigorous secular hagiography of Scots notables. Prosopography in the modern historiography of learning, focusing on the range of personnel in academic bodies, and their wider intellectual networks, rather than on isolated great men, has not challenged the substance of the patriotic case; it has merely lengthened the roll of honour.[14] Yet this one widely recognised Scoto-British contribution to modern Britain does nothing to bridge the disjunction between the personal triumphs of individual Scots and the general failures of the nation's independent economy and institutions, or to upset the prevailing Anglo-British interpretation of the rise of British liberty and prosperity.

The rise of a detached academic historiography in the twentieth century has not erased from the popular memory the tired and ideologically weak canon of patriotic shibboleths which survived the eighteenth- and nineteenth-century deconstruction of Scotland's historical myths. At the same time the increasing insulation of a university-based intellectual elite from the political nation has beset the very idea of a canon of Scottish history with new problems. These problems are not specific to Scotland, but have a particularly devastating impact on the historiography of a people trapped for so long in a limbo between nationhood and provinciality. J. H. Plumb has identified national chauvinism as one of the targets in an ideologically-charged 'past' under assault from a professionally-orientated 'history': 'The old past is dying . . . the historian should speed it on its way, for it was compounded of bigotry, of national vanity, of class domination . . . May history step into its shoes.' Yet this professional distancing can create crises of identity for nations whose historical courses have been much less troubled than Scotland's. One of Plumb's own protégés, David Cannadine, now laments that academic specialisation 'has often served not to illuminate the central themes of British history, but rather to obscure them', with a disconnected assortment of 'humdrum happenings' obliterating the 'major landmarks' and the 'high drama' of the coherent Whig narratives of English nationhood.[15]

We can also learn a great deal from the stimulating debate which these issues have provoked in Ireland, where national identity remains a central historical preoccupation. Irish historians divide into two broad schools: the proponents of either a detached value-free professionalism or its younger sibling, an iconoclastic revisionism, on the one hand, keen to abandon the 'tradition of writing the "story of Ireland" as a morality tale',[16] and on the other those who want a history which 'concedes nothing in the way of critical standards of scholarship', yet embraces 'empathy', 'imagination' and avoids 'filtering out the trauma' of Ireland's tragic history.[17] Where this debate impinges most directly on national historical canons is in the suggestion of one of the most articulate anti-nationalist revisionists, Steve Ellis, that the conception of a continuous national past is a notion flawed by anachronism. For instance, Ireland in the late medieval era, when the island was divided into a Gaelic territory and the Anglo-Norman Pale, is better described by the trans-national concept of 'borderlands'.[18] Brendan Bradshaw, the leading counter-revisionist, fears that emphasis on discontinuity, hybridity within the nation, and trans-national affinities without, undermines a 'holistic conception' of the national past; instead, 'the course of Irish history fragments into a series of more or less discrete epochs, each presenting a unique social, cultural and political configuration'.[19]

Scottish history, with its ethnic diversity, Highland-Lowland divide, borderlands, and regional involvement in Scandinavian and Irish political systems, appears similarly vulnerable. Scottish scholars are aware of the related modern interpretive tendencies towards disaggregating the national experience, while simultaneously absorbing the universalist perspectives of social science. The sociologist David McCrone has shown how the social peculiarities of small stateless nations like Scotland have been neglected by the tendency of sociology as a discipline to extrapolate unacknowledged the concepts derived from the foundational studies of American social phenomena to the rest of western modernity unmediated by an awareness of national difference. In addition, Michael Fry, the Tory-devolutionist historian, has drawn attention to the way in which the popularity of social and economic history in the historical profession is a threat to the idea of national history. Demographic perspectives, local studies whose rationale is the investigation of sub-national diversity, and emphasis on such western universals as class and industrialisation, do seem to undermine the very idea of the national historical experience. Recently such approaches have been used to demolish the myth of superior Scottish literacy in the early modern period. However, socioeconomic perspectives tend to dissolve other national solipsisms, not only Scotland's. Keith Wrightson has argued that the new social history, by deconstructing England as well as Scotland, has revealed the pluralism of 'many Englands and many Scotlands' which reflect the 'curious cultural constellation of British identity'.[20]

The revisionist currents in modern British historiography do in fact indicate that the outlook for Scottish history is less bleak than Fry fears. The loss of faith in the old canon of historical shibboleths occurred at a particular conjunction in the histories of ideas and political culture. In the mid eighteenth century the rise of the idea of progress in historical writing coincided with the ascendancy of Anglicisation in Scottish ideologies of economic improvement, anti-feudal reform and patriotic renewal. Anglicisation was equated with social evolution, in a qualified sense by the leading and sceptical historical sociologists of the Scottish Enlightenment, but more crudely in the rest of the political nation. In the English Whig histories of the last two centuries, the history of England obliterated the histories of Wales and Scotland, and to a lesser extent, Ireland, as the histories of backward societies now incorporated in the English story, whose pasts at any stage were of no particular interest as they were mere variants of that of the English vanguard-nation at an earlier period. But now English historical revisionists repent particularly of the sins of Anglocentricity and teleology, and have constructed new frameworks of interpretation within which Scots as well as English can recover pasts upon which more honest patriotisms might be founded. Scottish history has been liberated from English condescension, and the value of Scottish achievements can be assessed in a broader comparative perspective than that supplied by the former legend of English priorism. Only by understanding the collapse of this old English or Anglo-British Whig mythology can we properly locate the patriotic significance of the revisionist transformation of Scottish historiography.

Moreover, although the recent Scottish historical renaissance is largely autonomous and source-driven, it rests on unspoken theoretical assumptions about historical interpretation. The ultimate founding grandfathers of Scottish revisionism were not Scottish, and subscribed to a very different ideological outlook from most current historians of Scotland. Sir Herbert Butterfield, the architect of Peterhouse Toryism, in his classic work, *The Whig Interpretation of History* (1931), attacked the teleological assumptions which underlay presentist and progressive histories of the sort which had relegated the course of Scottish history to a position of unimportance in the unfolding of the glories of British liberalism and prosperity. Sir Lewis Namier launched a different Tory assault on the myths of Whig-liberal teleology. Namier penetrated beyond the superficially rational dimensions of political behaviour, unmasking high principles as 'flapdoodle' which disguised the seamier realities of politics, and exploding myths of constitutional and party evolution which obscured a substratum of self-interested political connections.[21]

Although Namierism was Tory in its original conception, its Scottish variant has probed the legitimacy of the Union of 1707. William Ferguson and P. W. J. Riley, who introduced Namierite analysis into Scottish historiography, have exploded the anodyne legend of Union as a disinterested act of far-sighted British statesmanship, and have not been reluctant to expose the sordid high-political dealings, and actual bribery, involved in the sacrifice, largely under the direction of the Scottish aristocracy, of the kingdom's autonomous political institutions.[22]

A former pupil of Butterfield's, J. G. A. Pocock, a post-imperial New Zealander cast adrift from his 'British' – and, he stresses, not simply English – heritage by European integration, has suggested, wistfully, but with great historical insight, that English historians reorient their discipline as the history of the British 'archipelago'. Pocock's suggestion, fertilised by H. G. Koenigsberger's analysis of the seventeenth-century Stuart realms as a 'composite monarchy', has borne fruit in the work of Conrad Russell. Scion of a Whig dynasty and himself a Liberal Democrat peer, Russell has contributed to the deconstruction of his own heritage by demolishing the Anglocentric and Whiggish framework of the English Revolution of the 1640s, transforming it into a religious war of the three kingdoms – England, Scotland, and Ireland – of the Stuart composite monarchy. No longer can the story of England's constitutional evolution be told as a domestic liberal legend; rather the central dynamics of this history are the multicultural British Isles and illiberal confessional politics. Nor can the smooth procession of English liberal values and institutions be so baldly and complacently contrasted with the intestine broils and religious fanaticism of Scottish and Irish histories.[23]

The dissolution of English Whig myths has also had repercussions on earlier periods. The caricature of late medieval Scottish history as sterile and devoid of significant parliamentary or centralising developments depended on a stark contrast with Stubb's English Whig myth of a Lancastrian constitutional experiment, and the successor-myth of bureaucratic state-building advanced by T. F. Tout. The emphases in the work of K. B. McFarlane and his successors on magnate retinues, systems of clientage – a revised 'bastard feudalism' – and the instability of English politics, particularly in the localities, have led to a demythologised reappraisal of late medieval England which complements the dismantling, by Jenny Wormald, Norman Macdougall and Sandy Grant, of the legend of late medieval Scotland as a benighted magnate anarchy. Scottish medieval state-building and constitutional development are now seen as 'different' rather than backward. In particular, Scotland is now reckoned to have made great strides in cohering as a political community, and even English scholars are beginning to recognise the Declaration of Arbroath as 'the most eloquent statement of regnal solidarity to come out of the middle ages'.[24]

Traditional concepts in economic history, such as English exceptionalism, and the Agricultural and Industrial Revolutions, have also come under assault. A story of continuity and of piecemeal development reigns in English economic history. For instance, N. F. R. Crafts has argued that growth rates in eighteenth-century England were of the same order as those in *ancien régime* France.[25] This reassessment of English economic achievements dovetails with the recent sensitivity to continuities in Scottish economic development, particularly in the works of Ian Whyte, Tom Devine and Robert Dodgshon. Cutting hyperbolic interpretations of the English Agrarian and Industrial Revolutions down to size reinforces the argument of these revisionists that the economic triumphs of late eighteenth-century Scotland drew on deep domestic roots. This argument substantially qualifies the propaganda advanced by enlightened anti-feudalist improvers in the mid eighteenth century that Scottish economic problems were a by-product of defects in the nation's feudal institutions and legal system and could only be remedied by Anglicization. Whyte and Dodgshon have exploded the myth of the eighteenth-century improvers and anti-feudalists that the Scottish agricultural sector was backward and resistant to innovation, by pointing to a variety of seventeenth-century successes.[26] This argument has been reinforced by Scottish demographers who are sceptical about the traditional mortality figures for the exceptional famine of the late 1690s, preferring, instead of a national picture of 30% mortality, one of a 5–15% fall in population, which includes emigration and a reduction in births.[27] Devine has challenged the argument that the modernising of eighteenth-century Scotland was predicated on incorporating Union with England; rather, he suggests, it depended to a large degree on the existing 'texture' of Scottish society.[28]

In the sphere of intellectual history, the situation has, of course, been less desperate. Scottish successes in philosophy, medicine and the natural sciences were well established and accorded their due. Recently, the reification of a wide range of eighteenth-century intellectual and cultural achievements as the 'Scottish Enlightenment' has not only strengthened this dimension of patriotic history, but has also stimulated a great deal of interest in Scotland throughout the international academic community. Yet, being so intimately associated with Union, Anglicisation and the assimilation of Scots to North Britishness, the Scottish Enlightenment sat uneasily in the patriotic canon. Ironically, it was Hugh Trevor-Roper, a Northumbrian keenly aware of his ancestral duty to harry the Scots, who inadvertently kindled patriotic interest in the pre-Union roots of the Scottish Enlightenment. Although Trevor-Roper was critical of seventeenth-century Scottish backwardness, nevertheless, by denigrating the presbyterian contribution to Scottish intellectual life, he drew attention to the rich but unexplored episcopalian culture of Restoration Scotland. Trevor-Roper also emphasised the role of Scotland's Continental diaspora culture in the transmission of ideas, suggesting an alternative diffusionist pathway to Enlightenment which by-passed Anglicisation.[29]

Emphasis on change, albeit non-revolutionary in the political sphere, and a teleology whose endpoint was wherever the course of English history had reached, were the hallmarks of evolutionary Whig historiography. The absorption of the methods of the social sciences, and particularly anthropology, into historical research has led to a new interest in enduring underlying structures in pre-modern Scottish society. Dodgshon, Wormald and Keith Brown have all adopted anthropological insights with conspicuous success, concentrating on the functioning of social systems in the past and their creative adaptation to contingencies and historical trends.[30] Moreover, Scotland is no longer directly and unfavourably compared with England. A wider range of comparisons with continental Europe, Ireland and Scandinavia is replacing the sterile question of how Scotland matched up to the standards set by her southern neighbour.[31]

Thus, despite the apparent desiccation and ideological barrenness of modern academic historiography, there are messages to be deciphered which might provide useful civic instruction, consolation, and perhaps even inspiration to the people of Scotland in their present predicament. Nor are modern Scots shackled to a national identity located in an imaginary Highlands and dressed in a kitsch tartanry. Again Trevor-Roper has been unintentionally inspirational, debunking the historical myth, while other historians have begun to expose tartanry's masquerade of sentimental Jacobite patriotism as but an obfuscation of both Scotland's participation in Empire and the undoubted excesses involved in the capitalist transformation of the Highlands.[32] Nor, in the light of the late Gordon Donaldson's scrupulous work on the Scottish Reformation, is a narrowly presbyterian nationalism viable.[33] Scottish historians have created an opportunity for Scots to cast off the residue of the old historical myths, and to construct a patriotism appropriate to the nation Scotland has become: a nation which, while being ill at ease with British nationalism of the Greater England variety, is nonetheless too much a part of western modernity to find implausible myths more edifying than the conclusions of a Scottish historical profession integrated with academic historiography in England and the United States, not exclusively dominated by Scots, and responsive to developments in other areas in the humanities and social sciences; a nation keen to preserve its own identity, but at the risk neither of violence on the scale of Bosnia or Northern Ireland, nor of detachment from the European Community. Modern Scottish historiography does not satisfy those who crave the romantic historical myths which fuel atavistic hatreds, but it does justice to Scotland's historical experience. It pays due recognition to our economic and cultural successes – and recent failures. It tells the story of how a people embroiled in intestine commotions throughout the late medieval and early modern periods evolved a cohesive and open national civil society very different from the tribal solidarities of other ethnic groups: in other words, although part of a larger composite state, Scotland achieved an authentic nationhood transcending mere ethnicity.[34] ❧

All Souls College, Oxford

1 See D. Deletant and H. Hanak (eds.), *Historians as Nation-Builders: Central and South-East Europe* (Houndmills: Macmillan, 1988), esp. articles by Clogg, Pearton and Pynsent, on Greek, Romanian and Czech historical traditions; R. F. Foster, 'History and the Irish Question', *Transactions of the Royal Historical Society* 5th series 33 (1983), 169–92 (pp. 187, 191–92); E. Niederhauser, 'Problèmes de la conscience historique dans les mouvements de renaissance nationale en Europe orientale', *Acta Historica* 18 (Budapest, 1972), 39–71 (p.69).

2 Geoffrey of Monmouth, *The History of the Kings of Britain*, trans. by L. Thorpe (Harmondsworth: Penguin, 1966); John of Fordun, *Chronica Gentis Scotorum* ed. by W. F. Skene (Edinburgh, 1871; with companion translation, Edinburgh, 1872)

3 E. J. Cowan, 'Myth and Identity in Early Medieval Scotland', *Scottish Historical Review* 63 (1984), 111–35; M. Drexler, 'Fluid Prejudice: Scottish Origin Myths in the Later Middle Ages', in J. Rosenthal and C. Richmond (eds.), *People, Politics and Community in the Later Middle Ages* (Gloucester: Alan Sutton, 1987); R. A. Mason, 'Scotching the Brut: Politics, History and National Myth in Sixteenth-Century Britain', in R. A. Mason (ed.) *Scotland and England 1286–1815* (Edinburgh: John Donald, 1987).

4 W. Ferguson, 'Imperial Crowns: A neglected facet of the background to the Treaty of Union of 1707', *Scottish Historical Review* 53 (1974), 22–44; C. Kidd, *Subverting Scotland's Past: Scottish Whig Historians and the Creation of an Anglo-British Identity 1689–c.1830* (Cambridge: CUP, 1993), chs. ii–iii, v.

5 A. A. M. Duncan, 'Hector Boece and the Medieval Tradition', in *Scots Antiquaries and Historians* (Abertay Historical Society, 16, Dundee, 1972); I. D. McFarlane, *Buchanan* (London: Duckworth, 1981), pp. 392–440.

6 R. A. Mason, 'Kingship and Commonweal: Political Thought and Ideology in Reformation Scotland' (unpubd doctoral thesis, Univ. of Edinburgh, 1983); D. Duncan, *Thomas Ruddiman* (Edinburgh: Oliver and Boyd, 1965).

7 Kidd, *Subverting Scotland's Past*, ch. iv.

8 Thomas Innes, *Critical Essay on the Ancient Inhabitants of the Northern Parts of Britain, or Scotland* (1729: Edinburgh, 1879).

9 Kidd, *Subverting Scotland's Past*, chs. vi–ix.

10 N. T. Phillipson, 'Nationalism and Ideology', in J. N. Wolfe (ed.), *Government and Nationalism in Scotland* (Edinburgh: EUP, 1969), p. 186.

11 M. Ash, *The Strange Death of Scottish History* (Edinburgh: Ramsay Head Press, 1980).

12 Thomas Urquhart, *Ekskubalauron: Or, The Discovery of a Most Exquisite Jewel* (1652), in Urquhart, *Works* (Maitland Club, Edinburgh, 1834); Dr George Mackenzie, *The Lives and Characters of the Most Eminent Writers of the Scots Nation* (3 vols., Edinburgh, 1708–22); C. Kidd, 'The Ideological Significance of Scottish Jacobite Latinity', in J. Black and J. Gregory (eds.), *Politics and Culture in Britain, 1660–1800* (Manchester: Manchester Univ. Press, 1991).

13 Hume to Gilbert Elliot, 2 July, 1757, in *The Letters of David Hume*, ed. by J. Y. T. Greig (2 vols., Oxford, 1932), i. 255; John Millar, *An Historical View of the English Government* (1787: 4 vols., London, 1803), iii. 86–94.

14 A. and N. Clow, *The Chemical Revolution* (London: Batchworth, 1952); A. Chitnis, *The Scottish Enlightenment and Early Victorian English Society* (London: Croom Helm, 1986).

15 J. H. Plumb, *The Death of the Past* (1969: Boston: Little, Brown, 1970), p. 145; D. Cannadine, 'British History: Past, Present – and Future?', *Past and Present* 116 (1987), 169–91 (p. 183).

16 R. F. Foster, *Modern Ireland 1600–1972* (1988: Harmondsworth: Penguin, 1989), p. ix.

17 B. Bradshaw, 'Nationalism and historical scholarship in modern Ireland', *Irish Historical Studies* 26 (1989), 329–51 (pp. 338, 350).

18 S. Ellis, 'Nationalist historiography and the English and Gaelic worlds in the late middle ages', *Irish Historical Studies* 25 (1986), 1–18.

19 Bradshaw, 'Nationalism and historical scholarship' (p. 346).

20 D. McCrone, *Understanding Scotland: The Sociology of a Stateless Nation* (London: Routledge, 1992); M. Fry, 'The Whig Interpretation of Scottish History', in I. Donnachie and C. Whatley (eds.), *The Manufacture of Scottish History* (Edinburgh: Polygon, 1992), p. 88; R. A. Houston, *Scottish Literacy and the Scottish Identity* (Cambridge: CUP, 1985); K. E. Wrightson, 'Kindred adjoining kingdoms: an English perspective on the social and economic history of early modern Scotland', in R. A. Houston and I. D. Whyte (eds.), *Scottish Society 1500–1800* (Cambridge: CUP, 1989), pp. 258, 260.

21 L. Colley, *Lewis Namier* (London: Weidenfeld and Nicolson, 1989); L. Namier, *The Structure of Politics at the Accession of George III* (1929: 2nd edn, London: Macmillan, 1957); Namier, *England in the Age of the American Revolution* (1930: 2nd edn, London: Macmillan, 1961).

22 P. W. J. Riley, 'The Parliament of 1703', *Scottish Historical Review* 47 (1968), 129–50; Riley, *King William and the Scottish Politicians* (Edinburgh: John Donald, 1979); Riley, *The Union of England and Scotland* (Manchester: Manchester Univ. Press, 1978); W. Ferguson, *Scotland's Relations with England: a Survey to 1707* (Edinburgh: John Donald, 1977); Ferguson, 'The Making of the Treaty of Union of 1707', *Scottish Historical Review* 43 (1964), 89–110.

23 J. G. A. Pocock, *The Limits and Divisions of British History*, Studies in Public Policy 31, Univ. of Strathclyde (Glasgow, 1979); H. G. Koenigsberger, '*Dominium Politicum* or *Dominium Politicum et Regale*: Monarchies and Parliaments in Early Modern Europe' (1975), in Koenigsberger, *Politicians and Virtuosi* (London: Hambledon Press, 1986); C. Russell, *The Causes of the English Civil War* (Oxford: OUP, 1990); Russell, *The Fall of the British Monarchies 1637–42* (Oxford: OUP, 1991).

24 K. B. McFarlane, *Lancastrian Kings and Lollard Knights* (Oxford: OUP, 1972); McFarlane, *The Nobility of Later Medieval England* (Oxford: OUP, 1973); S. Reynolds, *Kingdoms and Communities in Western Europe, 900–1300* (1984: Oxford: OUP, 1990 pbk), p. 274; J. M. Brown (now Wormald) (ed.), *Scotland in the Fifteenth Century* (London: Edward Arnold, 1977), esp. articles by Brown (Wormald) and Macdougall; A. Grant, *Independence and Nationhood – Scotland 1306–1469* (London: Edward Arnold, 1984); Grant, 'The Middle Ages: the Defence of Independence', in R. Mitchison (ed.), *Why Scottish History Matters* (Saltire Society, 1991), p. 22; G. W. S. Barrow, 'The idea of freedom in late medieval Scotland', *Innes Review* 30 (1979), 16–34.

25 N. F. R. Crafts, 'Industrial Revolution in England and France: Some Thoughts on the Question, "Why was England First?"', *Economic History Review* 2nd series 30 (1977), 429–41; E. Kerridge, *The Agricultural Revolution* (London, 1967). See also, D. Cannadine, 'The Present and the Past in the English Industrial Revolution 1880–1980', *Past and Present* 103 (1984), 131–72 (pp. 132, 162, 165–66).

26 I. D. Whyte, *Agriculture and Society in Seventeenth-century Scotland* (Edinburgh: John Donald, 1979); R. A. Dodgshon, *Land and Society in Early Scotland* (Oxford: OUP, 1981); see also C. Beveridge and R. Turnbull, *The Eclipse of Scottish Culture* (Edinburgh: Polygon, 1989), esp. ch iii.

27 T. C. Smout, 'The ill years of the 1690s', in M. W. Flinn (ed.), *Scottish population history from the 17th century to the 1930s* (Cambridge: CUP, 1977), pp. 180–81; R. E. Tyson, 'Famine

in Aberdeenshire, 1695–99', in D. Stevenson (ed.), *From Lairds to Louns: Country and Burgh Life In Aberdeenshire, 1600–1800* (Aberdeen: AUP, 1986).

28 T. M. Devine, 'The Union of 1707 and Scottish Development', *Scottish Economic and Social History* 5 (1985), 23–40 (p. 37).

29 H. R. Trevor-Roper, 'The Scottish Enlightenment', *Studies on Voltaire and the Eighteenth Century* lviii (1967), 1635–58. For the native pre-Union roots of the Scottish Enlightenment, see also G. Donaldson, 'Stair's Scotland: The Intellectual Inheritance', *Juridical Review* (1981), 128–45; R. H. Campbell and A. S. Skinner (eds.), *The Origins and Nature of the Scottish Enlightenment* (Edinburgh: John Donald, 1982); R. L. Emerson, 'Sir Robert Sibbald, Kt., the Royal Society of Scotland and the Origins of the Scottish Enlightenment', *Annals of Science* 45 (1988), 41–72.

30 R. A. Dodgshon, ' "Pretense of Blude" and "Place of Thair Duelling": The Nature of Scottish Clans, 1500–1745', in Houston and Whyte (eds.), *Scottish Society 1500–1800*; J. Wormald, 'Bloodfeud, Kindred, and Government in Early Modern Scotland', *Past and Present* 87 (1980), 54–97; Keith Brown, *Bloodfeud in Scotland 1573–1625: Violence, Justice and Politics in an Early Modern Society* (Edinburgh: John Donald, 1986).

31 See, e.g., R. Mitchison, *The Roots of Nationalism: Studies in Northern Europe* (Edinburgh: John Donald, 1980); T. Devine and D. Dickson (eds.), *Ireland and Scotland, 1600–1850* (Edinburgh: John Donald, 1983); T. C. Smout (ed.), *Scotland and Europe, 1200–1850* (Edinburgh: John Donald, 1986); G. Simpson (ed.), *Scotland and Scandinavia, 800–1800* (Edinburgh: John Donald, 1990).

32 H. R. Trevor-Roper, 'The Highland Tradition of Scotland', in E. Hobsbawm and T. Ranger (eds.), *The Invention of Tradition* (Cambridge: CUP, 1983); P. Womack, *Improvement and Romance: Constructing the Myth of the Highlands* (Houndmills: Macmillan, 1989).

33 G. Donaldson, *The Scottish Reformation* (Cambridge: CUP, 1960), ch. v.

34 I should like to thank Jenny Wormald and John Robertson for commenting on this essay. To a greater degree than is usual on such occasions, I must stress that they bear no responsibility for the opinions expressed.

MARSHALL WALKER

The age of the periphery: an ex-paranoiac's thoughts on the literary canon

A *Times Literary Supplement* 'Commentary' on Jacques Derrida's visit to Oxford in March 1992 refers to 'the long afternoon of theory'.[1] If early 1992 was that afternoon, the International Association of University Professors of English conference at York in 1986 must have met about high noon. Critical paths from across the world led to the gates of the walled city, but when you got there the old guide-books were useless. Familiar avenues of discourse were blocked by the heavy machineries of deconstruction and roads up without prospect of being resurfaced. Amid the din and dust of drills and shovels wielded by the academic muscle-men in their frayed Lévi-Strausses could be heard nervous talk of the canon. It was a problem, it was a figment, it was a lesser dinosaur scarcely meriting taxidermy, it was, like God and the family, an obsolete institution as irrelevant as Galsworthy and the first 'Pomp and Circumstance' march in a world of Rushdie and Schnittke. It was phallocentric and élitist, arbitrary, honky, *pakeha* and imperialist, sepia-tinted, doomed. A canon implies 'Great Books', but great books are not the only books, and who pronounces them great anyway? After all, even Shakespeare's inclusion in the canon has not always been secure. In 1814 Byron wrote to James Hogg 'Shakespeare's name, you may depend on it, stands absurdly too high and will go down'.[2]

In 1986 at York the canon, clearly, was shot; and at the end of the conference the richly inconclusive Frank Kermode tentatively led his congregation in something close to obsequy. 'It may be', he said, 'that Puerto Ricans should not be made to read Shakespeare'.

Subfusc and defunctive, the authority of the canon would yield to the preferences of the consumer. The market would adjudicate on quality. A stout British empirical tradition was there for support, notably in Dr Johnson for whom, 'in questions that relate to the heart of man', the ultimate arbiter was 'the common voice of the multitude, uninstructed by precept and unprejudiced by authority'.[3] In the global village the multitude included Puerto Ricans, Indians and West Indians, Africans, Polynesians, Japanese, the European Community, Scots, Irish and Welsh, gays, feminists, green-earthers, save-the-whalers, and members of the Volkswagen Club of America, vegetarian section. The canon hadn't a hope. Jane Austen and Dickens move over for Anita Brookner and Albert Wendt, *Ulysses* for Keri Hulme's Booker-prized *The Bone People*, Forster for Narayan, Conrad for Achebe. Milton and Wordsworth, Whitman and Dickinson, the British Victorians, Eliot and Stevens disappear behind a curtain of confessionals from Lowell, Berryman, Plath and Sexton which in its turn shreds under the onslaught of poetry-circuit bards free-versing earnest, mediocre egos at literary soirées and festivals from Aberdeen to Adelaide, hearts, lungs and livers trembling on their denim sleeves.

Are we stuffily to complain about these new, evidently rampant market values? There is more to them than the cynicism of film-makers who know which semiotics will sell, more than cultural bigotry or academic failure of nerve. There is no gainsaying the truth of the introduction to *Braided Lives*, a recent anthology of multicultural American writing:

> People become avid readers when they find personal meaning in litera-ture. We read with conviction, commitment, and motivation those works that reflect our own experiences or histories or speak to us in ways that are real and true. The stories and poems in this volume attest to the surprise and wonder of finding these connections between literature and life. As the storyteller in James Baldwin's 'Sonny's Blues' discovers, 'For while the tale of how we suffer and how we are delighted and how we may triumph is never new, it always must be heard'.[4]

Among the variations of the eternal tale offered by the anthology are stories by Zora Neale Hurston, James Baldwin, Alice Walker, Nikki Giovanni and Maxine Hong Kingston as well as work by new, emerging writers; so the shibboleth, relevance, need be neither *parvenu* nor cheapskate. And who would quarrel with the *raison d'être* of the collection to instil an appetite for literature by providing 'personal meaning' through reflections of 'experiences or histories . . . that are real and true'?

The *Braided Lives* anthology's recourse to the allure of recognition shows due respect for Wordsworth's 'grand elementary principle of pleasure' by which a human being 'knows, and feels, and lives, and moves'. Would we beat a Trinidadian into linguistic and theological despair with Milton's account of man's first disobedience when he can have Naipaul's *A House for Mr Biswas* or *A Bend in the River*? Would we oppress an Indian with Hardy's fateful Anglo-Saxon Wessex or Faulkner's guilt-humid Yoknapatawpha when there are the streets of Narayan's Malgudi to feel comfortable in? Would we sentence a woman to Browning, Conrad and Hemingway when there are Emily Dickinson, George Eliot, Kate Chopin, Katherine Mansfield, Nadine Gordimer, Margaret Atwood and Liz Lochhead? To turn the question round, is it not salutary that Miltonists should know the work of the Trinidadian, that the Englishman's heath should make way for a South Indian town, and is it not high time that the visions of women should command the belated respect of readers of all kinds, complexions and degrees? Would not we all, if the truth be told, prefer to curl up with Wilson Harris or Toni Morrison than with Dryden?

Post-imperialist things fall apart; the old centre cannot and should not hold. This sort of deconstruction rules by the energy of new and freshly discovered literatures which makes new centres out of old peripheries. And how solid was the centre anyway? Change was crucial to Eliot's famous model in 'Tradition and the Individual Talent'[5] and the existing monuments are even more susceptible to change than he suggests. A work of the past, rediscovered and revalued, can change the old order as profoundly as a new work. We know this from the impact, perhaps unprecedented, of Grierson's epoch-making edition of the poems of Donne in 1912. Or, to go to another art, we may notice an adjustment to our perception of twentieth-century Russian music as a consequence of the increased attention recently accorded the operas and sonatas of Prokofiev, a different sense of his relation to Shostakovich and of the co-ordinates of Soviet musical culture. The conductor Neeme Järvi's revelation of the music of his fellow Estonian, Eduard Tubin, has subtly altered our former sense of the 'ideal order' of the previously held canon of twentieth-century symphonists from Mahler to Sibelius, Nielsen and Bax and the astonishing popular success of Henryk Górecki's Third Symphony has altered it again.

New works and new assessments of old works, as well as new countries and continents of works, inevitably bring change. But does change necessarily mean decay? Janice Mirikitani, a third-generation Japanese American, says, 'Words from the Third World are like food. Universal, essential, procreative, freeing, connective, satisfying'.[6] There can be no objection to this as personal testimony in which many may find a general truth. The trouble starts when such a statement is admitted as evidence that words from the Old World are by definition opposite in quality, lacking in nutrition, parochial, superficial, sterile, constricting, divisive and therefore obsolete.

Just such implications provided the fusillade that brought down the 'Western Culture' course taught at Stanford University. Stanford required that all first-year students read from a standard list of classics of Western thought. After some two years of discussion during which this marmoreal course was attacked by feminists, advocates of minority literatures, deconstructionists and other leftist persuasions, a new course was adopted to replace 'Western Culture'. The new course apparently retained six works from the original list of 'classics' – the Bible, Plato, St Augustine, Machiavelli, Rousseau and Marx – but also included the study of at least one non-European culture and undertook to pay 'attention to issues of race, gender and class'. For the inflexible American Secretary of Education, William Bennett, the changes meant that a great university had been brought low by the very forces which 'modern universities came into being to oppose – ignorance, irrationality and intimidation'.[7] From being a transmitter of culture Stanford had become a time-serving advocate of ascendant political agendas. William Chace, Professor of English and Stanford's vice-provost for academic planning, defended the new course with dignity: 'This pedagogical step was taken on the basis of the recognition, hardly radical, that "issues of race, gender and class" deeply affect the world in which we live and in which our forbears lived. Others might wish to think that such matters make no difference to cultural formation, but they might find themselves mistaken'.[8]

Game, set and match to Professor Chace, it might seem. Nevertheless there are works which make up a canon of enduring significance. They may be accounted great because, like the Bible, they have shaped cultures and made a special impact on the English language. They may be great because, like the writings of Machiavelli and Marx, they propound seminal theories of political practices and the anatomy of society, or they may be great, like Shakespeare, because they take the raw and random material of life and order it by the shaping power of imagination in language of matchless precision, poetry and power. The American historian, Gertrude Himmelfarb, straightforwardly supports the traditional curriculum: 'It used to be thought that ideas transcend race, gender and class, that there are such things as truth, reason, morality and artistic excellence, which can be understood and aspired to by everyone, of whatever race, gender or class'.[9] To this Walter Jackson Bate succinctly adds, 'No one believes in greatness. That's gone'.[10]

Having rejected God we proceed to topple other eminences and our self-sufficiency expands to fill the void we make. The author, too, is dead, according to Roland Barthes and his formidable diaspora; the mini-god from whom a text formerly emanated is dismissed by the egalitarian subversives of contemporary theory as a merely historical idea formulated by and appropriate to the social beliefs of democratic, capitalistic society with its emphasis on the individual. Where there were once works of literary art there are now only relativistic 'texts'; where until recently literature was considered a high point of human achievement, 'it is now said to be a record of self-delusion and sinister attempts by the haves to propagandize the have-nots'.[11] It has been an olympic decline, from zenith to nadir in less than thirty years.

Some acts of demolition are admirably motivated by a considered belief

that a given eminence is outmoded or decayed and by a constructive determination, in Ezra Pound's phrase, to 'make it new' – a sort of intellectual
slum-clearance. Others arise from a failure to understand the continuity of
human effort, which includes the continuity of human error, and the nature
of tradition. For the educated person tradition is not an option; it is inescap-
able. Stanford's 'Western Culture' syllabus prescribed works of the past that
made the intellectual, political, moral, aesthetic and linguistic present in
which we live now. These works formed the cultural milieu in which the new
literatures in English are, happily, exploding and their relevance is incontro-
vertibly a fact for the non-English Briton, the African or the Hispanic
American or the Indian or the Australian who writes in English because the
language, in the state in which he or she picks it up, has been formed by the
past. 'The English language has been taken over', says Vikram Seth, 'or taken
to heart, or taken to tongue, by people whose original language historically
it was not'.[12] True, but to call a work 'epic' still invokes Homer, Virgil and
their Christianized amplification in Milton; to call a work 'lyrical' implies a
relation to the sonnet and to Wordsworth and Coleridge; the term 'tragic'
carries a frame of reference that originates with the Greeks but is dominated
by the Shakespearean form. To have a feeling for style requires a sense of the
map of styles: the kennings and half-line tensions of *Beowulf*; the speed, wit
and fullness of Chaucer; the plain-speaking of the Geneva Bible and the
orotundities of the Authorized Version; the demotic of Burns and the snap of
Pope; the poetic diction against whose antimacassar decadence Wordsworth
took so effective a stand in one generation, Pound, Eliot and MacDiarmid in
another; the incisiveness and clamour of Dickens and the labyrinthine
savourings of Henry James; the sprung rhythms and alliterations of Hopkins,
Auden and Thomas. These are places from which Derridean quarks of
significance come irresistibly into the language.

Once a tool whereby peoples were brought to imperial heel, the English
language has become the peoples' possession. As George Steiner says, 'Democracy is, fundamentally, at odds with the canonic',[13] yet canonic
re-assertions are inevitable whenever standards are invoked. The canon that
was, is still, albeit with its pores open. It is not a matter of the canon versus
the new for the new is what it is because the canon was there first. Developing
and re-assessed cultures may produce works which penetrate, or overshadow
and diminish the works that comprise any canon. We must believe that they
will: it would be a counsel of despair to believe that we might not look forward
to higher forms of art, superior theories of society, subtler, more adequate
philosophies, sharper insights into politics, economics, aesthetics. Western
Civilization as it has been is a fact of history whether we like it or not, and
so are the works by which it is pillared, whether we choose to like them or
not; but there is more to 'Liberal Education' than its basic architecture. What

the canon has lost is its normative value, its imperious prescriptive force and its exclusivity. The canon's authority as fact no longer has the power to marginalize the outsider. Peripheries are asserting themselves in a global fugue of regional accents. Received Standard English, mercifully, is put out to grass, a museum piece, and even the BBC's World Service news-readers irradiate daily the intonations of Scotland and the North of England as well as the plummier tones of the Home Counties. 'Taggart' is a world-wide export success; Tom Leonard is read in Gdansk and Stellenbosch.

The canon's loss of its normative value as an index of Arnoldian touch-stones is liberating, but it also prompts new responsibilities. It is time for the peripheral culture to examine itself, undaunted by the canon and with the kind of love we should mean when we speak of patriotism. It must be a critical love, of course, and this is a real problem. Swift claimed he had 'reconcil'd Divinity and Wit', but can a way be found to reconcile love and criticism? Can a secessionist Scot forgive James Thomson for providing Thomas Arne with the words for 'Rule Britannia' in *The Masque of Alfred* or, if Robert Crawford is right, graduates of the Scottish academy for inventing 'Eng. Lit'?[14] But if patriotism is the last refuge of a scoundrel, it would be a squalid bolt-hole for a critic. Stepping out from the canon's intimidating shadow, retaining appropriate historical respect for it as formative fact but shaking off fear like a handful of dust, how might a patriotic Scot, for example, attempt the revaluation of his peripheral literary culture and the definition of a provisional national canon? Perhaps a sketch of an answer might offer some notes towards a model not only for Scots but for others who feel an obligation to do the same for their own places. The job requires a sense of the earth, a resolution to face the problem of stereotypes and a determination to find the special story the culture tells. How might the job be attempted for the allegedly post-colonial Scottish periphery?

A good Scottish authority, *Chambers Twentieth Century Dictionary*, defines a patriot as 'one who truly, or ostentatiously and injudiciously, loves and serves his fatherland'. The one who truly loves and serves now seems obsolete; in the currently popular use of the term a patriot is a Tory jingoist with a pipe in his mouth and a book by Kipling in his pocket. The word today is inseparable from the pejoration of Dr Johnson's apothegm, or else it signifies all the love of a guided war missile. Suppose, then, we risk the charge of *faux naïf*, turn the semantic clock back to love and service and consider the poem, 'Scotland', by Hugh MacDiarmid:

It requires great love of it deeply to read
The configuration of a land,
Gradually grow conscious of fine shadings,
Of great meanings in slight symbols,
Hear at last the great voice that speaks softly,
See the swell and fall upon the flank
Of a statue carved out in a whole country's marble,
Be like Spring, like a hand in a window
Moving New and Old things carefully to and fro,
Moving a fraction of flower here,
Placing an inch of air there,
And without breaking anything.[15]

This not only vindicates love but requires it. Love is needed to read 'deeply' (or, for the critic, adequately) the configuration of a land, that is, the filigree of a culture. Love is needed if there is to be an awareness of subtleties, 'fine shadings', as well as the homogeneity of the national culture, the 'statue carved out in a whole country's marble'. Love is needed if damage is not to accrue from the critical rearrangement of 'New and Old things'. In other words, the monuments can only be arranged competently in a literary history if the ordering is motivated and informed by love, and without love the discriminatory act will result in breakage.

Let us consider a piece of the whole marble of Scotland. The isle of Lismore is a sliver of land set in Loch Linnhe in Argyllshire. It lies off Port Appin to the north and is seven miles distant from Oban to the south. The Gaelic name means 'great garden'. A low-lying island, its chief marvel, ribbed by underlying folds of limestone, is its highest point, Bàrr Mòr ('Big Top'), a modest 417 feet high, from which may be seen the whole of the Great Glen from Ben Cruachan in the east to the hunched shoulder of Ben Nevis in the north and, southward, the Paps of Jura. The island has the remains of a galleried Pictish broch built some time after 500 BC, a Norse fortification of unknown date and Achnaduin Castle, a fourteenth-century building used by the bishops of Lismore. In 562 AD Moluag and Columba, natives of Ireland, arrived on the west coast of Scotland looking for a central place from which they might disseminate Christianity. Each chose Lismore and sought to be the first to land. Their coracles raced towards the island, oarsmen urged on by the two tonsured missionaries. As they approached the shore Moluag saw that his rival's boat would win. Picking up an axe, he placed his little finger on the gunwale, severed it from his hand, threw it on the shingle ahead and shouted, 'My flesh and blood have first possession of this island and I bless it in the name of the Lord'. Tradition has it that St Columba was a bad loser and cursed Moluag, saying, 'May you have the alder for your firewood'. Moluag answered with saintly equanimity, 'The Lord will make the alder burn pleasantly'. St Columba attacked again: 'May you have the jagged ridges for your pathway'. Still Moluag was beyond provocation and replied, 'The Lord will smooth them to the feet'. The pastoral staff of St Moluag, the Bachuil Mòr, a piece of blackthorn measuring two feet and nine inches, can still be seen on the island at the home of the Baron of Bachuil.[16]

In this piece of the configuration of Scotland a literary history might begin with a motivation legitimately born out of limestone furrows and the stones of Picts and Vikings, out of the staff of a resolute saint and the copse of alder trees at the bay where he landed, out of the congregation of peaks visible from the cairn of Bàrr Mòr. History is taken back to pre-plaid blood and bone, idealism, geology and landscape, rocks and stones and trees. Here are the promptings of particular earth to love and enquire, to want to know how imagination has risen to the measure of the country, its people, its history, its sense of itself. As MacDiarmid says in 'On a Raised Beach': 'We must reconcile ourselves to the stones, / Not the stones to us'. Sibelius once said to Bengt de Törne: 'When we see these granite rocks we know why we can treat the orchestra as we do'.[17] The connections between Ayrshire's subtle contours and the moods of Burns, or between the rigorous architectural grace of Edinburgh's New Town and the stiffness of Robert Louis Stevenson's prose, or between Norman MacCaig's love of Suilven and his essential laconism may be mysteries beyond the audacity of criticism. But the view from Bàrr Mòr is a summons to try to approach the Scottish imagination by way of its own fundamentally theological habit of taking things back to first principles.

Here, too, are promptings to look beyond stereotypical perceptions of the culture of the country and to be on guard against them when reading its literature. The clichés are all too familiar: the Scot is tight-fisted, brutish, maudlin, canny, repressed, volatile, alcoholic, dourly religious, a complex barbarian worth inspecting as one of the world's ethnic sideshows. Mary Queen of Scots, Bonnie Prince Charlie, shortbread, cabers and bagpipes, quaint accents, the bonnie banks of Loch Lomond and the Massacre of Glencoe make a culture colourful enough to sustain the kitsch-encrusted tourist industry whereby Scotland has colluded in its own inferiorization.[18] Clichés beget ignorance: the visitors come and ask their questions. In 1978 an Edinburgh tourist guide was moved to report samples. 'Excuse me', said one visitor to John Knox's house in Edinburgh's Royal Mile, 'but where did Knox keep the bodies he bought from Burke and Hare?' Talking of *Treasure Island* the guide remarked that Robert Louis Stevenson was sickly as a boy. 'My goodness', gushed a wide-eyed English lady, 'to think he grew up and invented the railway engine'. At Abbotsford one American visitor wanted to see the cloak the chivalrous knight spread out for Queen Elizabeth; another remarked that it sure was a big house for a ploughman to have lived in; and a third, doubtless wishing to highlight the ignorance of the other two, chipped in with: 'Did Scott really write all those books before he went to the South Pole?'.[19] Such fatuities imply the popularly held conception of a tartan canon: Knox, Burns, Scott and Stevenson.

On a higher plane of error Matthew Arnold, who never toured Scotland – and in 1877 declined nomination as Rector of the University of St Andrews – commends Burns for a view of the world that is 'large, free, shrewd, benignant – truly poetic, therefore', but finds that the poet, like Chaucer, falls short of the high seriousness of the great classics. This is hardly surprising in poetry which, Arnold says, deals 'perpetually with Scotch drink, Scotch religion, and Scotch manners'.[20] The drink needs no identifying, the manners derive therefrom and the religion is either bigoted Protestant, bigoted Papist or, in the west of Scotland, the transposition of these into the blue and the green, Rangers and Celtic, endemically clashing armies of an eternal cultural night. Calvin, certainly, has been more formative than the papal see, particularly since the Disruption of 1843. In the name of true Presbyterian values, the 'unco guid' of the Free Church invested the good life with a gloom even Calvin would have found over-rigid. The consequences are satirized by Charles, Lord Neaves, in what he calls 'A Lyric for Saturday Night':

> We zealots, made up of stiff clay,
>   The sour-looking children of sorrow,
> While not over-jolly today,
>   Resolve to be wretched tomorrow.
> We can't for a certainty tell
>   What mirth may molest us on Monday;
> But, at least, to begin the week well,
>   Let us all be unhappy on Sunday.

Arnold's 1880 assessment of Burns gives the impression of a mind programmed by the hackneyed triad before engagement with the poetry: he found what he expected to find, and the tartan-quilted gift-shop editions of Burns have perpetuated the sentimental cliché of the heaven-taught but wayward ploughman with too soft a spot for women and 'whisky gill or penny wheep'. To make matters worse, the impression of a national proclivity to drink, manners (uncouth) and religion can be reinforced by modern instances.

'Butcher Boiled His Friend', proclaimed the front page of the Glasgow Evening Times,[21] implying that England's Sweeney Todd had met his match at last. The butcher and his friend had been sharing a Friday evening pint. An argument led to the exchange of insults, then of blows. A pickaxe was introduced and the friend lay dead. The butcher put the folded body of his friend in the shop's boiler, went home for dinner, and returned to the scene of the crime intending to mince the remains. When the mincer proved too small he planned to take the body to his mother's house which was empty as she was on holiday. Remorse struck in the early hours of Sunday. He confessed to his employer who contacted the police. When the butcher's wife was invited to comment she was reported as saying, 'I can't understand how he came to kill Andy Kerr, with whom he was very friendly'. It is the Arnoldian triad again. The story begins with drink, descends to violent manners and dissipates in sabbath remorse to end with the impeccable grammatical manners of the wife's alleged 'with whom'.

An antidote may be found in a Glasgow pub. Clientele is mainly working class and drinking methodical. Lounge-bar niceties are spurned here; ladies are not banned as they were in the old days, but there are no wilting crisps, no soggy pickled onions. Men stand at the bar or sit at spartan tables, getting on with it. The pint glasses of 'Heavy' go up and down like the pistons of a Caledonian MacBrayne ferry plugging up the Sound of Mull. A big man comes in, orders a half of whisky and a pint. He wears brown dungarees, a cloth cap pushed back on his head, heavy boots. Twenty minutes later, outside three whiskies and three pints, he is forgetting the day's nipping winds on the building site. He begins to whistle, beating time to himself with his fingers on the counter. The man next to him at the bar turns his head.

'Heh, Jimmy, whit's that yer whistlin'?'

The big man doesn't seem to hear. He goes on whistling, fingers drumming, eyes fixed on the mirror behind the bar as though it reflects the grandeur he sees inside his head.

'Come on, Jimmy', the other man says, 'gie's the name o' yer tune'.

The whistling stops. The hand pauses in its drumming and a finger is pointed at the interlocutor.

'D'ye no recognise it, ma friend?'

'Nuh. Ah doan recognise it. 'S nice, but ah doan recognise it'.

'It's Sibelius, ma friend. Sibelius', the big man says, pronouncing the name in four majestically spaced chords. 'Sibelius, Symphony Nummer Twa. That's the last bit o' it. *Allegro moderato*'.

'Is that right?' says the other, vaguely impressed.

'Sibelius', says the big man. 'Magic. Sibelius is pure fuckin' magic'.[22]

The Scottish savage may be *Grand Guignol* like the butcher in his fateful flyting or, like the builder, a lord of culture even in his drink and the violence of his diction. Butcher and builder should remind us that one theme on which Scottish literary history offers a long series of variations is the lot of common people. There is, of course, a main vein of humane sympathy that comes up from Barbour through the moralizing of Henryson, the complaints or satires of Dunbar and Sir David Lyndsay's John the Common-Weill in *Ane Pleasant*

Satyre of the Thrie Estaitis; but a vigorous egalitarian strain becomes especially evident towards the end of the eighteenth century. Notwithstanding the influence of Tom Paine, Scottish writers were precociously in advance of the political radicals in works which refrain on the common good and the worth of the individual. The refrain can be heard in David Hume, Adam Smith and Henry Mackenzie.

While prose ran its enlightened course into social and political responsibility and the sense of Scotland in a rapidly changing world, poets too engaged with the lives of real people. Allan Ramsay's work is uneven but he put heart into the Scots language and his diverse activities crucially stimulated the influential cultural life of Edinburgh. His anthologies and his own poetry make a fresh, prophetic annunciation about the relation of the Scots language to landscape and life, preparing the way for a subsequent prophet in 'poor Bob Fergusson' and then the messiah, Robert Burns. Fergusson quickly found his feet as a writer when he abandoned the conventional manners of English pastoral in favour of Scots. Like Ramsay he loves his Edinburgh despite its gentry, castigating it for its dirt, smells and libertinism in 'Auld Reekie' but doing so from the inside with a Hogarthian relish of detail. Typically, affection and satire are combined in 'Braid Claith', where the fun the poet is having is evident in the way he plays with the six-line 'Standard Habbie' stanza in rhymes worthy of McGonagall:

> For thof ye had as wise a snout on
> As Shakespear or Sir Isaac Newton,
> Your judgement fouk wou'd hae a doubt on,
> > I'll tak my aith,
> Till they cou'd see ye wi' a suit on
> > O' gude Braid Claith.

Here the jocose Fergusson's satire on clothing as a measure of human worth anticipates Burns's more Swiftian contempt for 'tinsel show . . . silks . . . riband, star and a' that'. Fergusson enjoys the folly where Burns, within his comic vision, is scathing about the superficiality of rank in his affirmation of the radical ideas of liberty, equality and fraternity.

We can move on through Scottish writers, noticing the conservative Walter Scott's respect for the independence of ordinary people; James Hogg's anger towards the presbyterian establishment's persecution of the common folk; the arch-dominie Carlyle's sympathy for the plight of the untrustworthy masses; Margaret Oliphant's sensitive analysis of provincial life; James (Bysshe Vanolis) Thomson's Eliotesque vision of the city as an alienating dystopia in *The City of Dreadful Night*; George MacDonald's reformist compassion for the sufferings of the poor; John Davidson's social anger in 'Thirty Bob a Week'; accounts of working-class life in plays by Bill Bryden (*Willie*

Rough), Roddy McMillan (*The Bevellers*) and Tom McGrath (*The Hard Man*); the 7:84 Theatre Company's attack on feudalism and capitalism in John McGrath's *ceilidh*-style play, *The Cheviot, the Stag and the Black, Black Oil*; and the television mini-series, *Edge of Darkness*, Troy Kennedy Martin's realistic and mythopoeic exposé of nuclear-age capitalist cynicism towards the well-being of the planet in Thatcher's visigothic Britain. We can point to the democratic manifesto implicit in Tom Leonard's use of Glasgow *patois* to cut through to a real, placed company of flesh and blood. So Leonard protests, as Gaelic at its greater remove never could quite do, against the bending of a country's mind by 'a police régime of the signifier', to co-opt a phrase of Edward Said's,[23] that is, by the undemocratic authority of a language whose insidious 'correctness' derives from the bullying powers of Oxbridge élitism, a remote parliament and a still remoter throne. In a poem called 'Good Style' Leonard puns on the title phrase in its Scottish usage for 'vigorously or with flair' and its implication of poetic decorum. Setting out a poem in a phonetic rendering of the language of the people can make it difficult for the outsider. Leonard turns this into a gesture of defiance towards imagined objections by supercilious practitioners of 'standard English':

> helluva hard tay read theez init
> stull
> if yi canny unnirston thim jiss clear aff then
> gawn
> get tay fuck ootma road
>
> ahmaz goodiz thi lota yiz so ah um
> ah no whit ahm dayn
> tellnyi
> jiss try enny a yir fly patir wi me
> stick thi bootnyi good style
> so ah wull

Given Roderick Watson's comprehensive and judicious literary history of 1984,[24] why should new evaluations of Scottish literature be called for now? Justification is partly in the changes of structures and attitudes seen in this last quarter of the twentieth century. These include the altered status of the canon as well as changes only recently comprehensible in the nature of society from the decline of the aristocracy so meticulously charted by David Cannadine in *The Decline and Fall of the British Aristocracy*[25] to the rise of minority groups and the impact of feminism. Even more vividly immediate are changes quite suddenly visible in the political map of the world: the 'end of the American century', the rise of global cities as command points in the organization of world economy, and the supremely dramatic collapse of the Soviet

Union into its constituent parts with all that this process implies for the autonomy of the smaller national unit whether Lithuania, Wales, Bosnia-Herzegovina or Scotland. Culturally, in the turning world, there are no still points because history does not permit them. Under the impact of such changes it is time for Scots to look at themselves afresh and to encourage others to join in the scrutiny. As Edwin Morgan says, 'CHANGE RULES is the supreme graffito'.[26] A cartoon portrayal of change in Scotland over the last decade might be expressed by a progression from the drunk, dour and feckless butcher with his incongruously grammatical wife to the equally indigenous but buoyantly integrated builder whistling Sibelius's Second Symphony after three whiskies, blending Tom Leonard's 'good-style' diction with high art, no mere noble savage but a real person ready for 1990 when his Glasgow will be proclaimed 'European City of Culture'. Here G. Gregory Smith's 'Caledonian Antisyzygy' is resurgent in a new harmony, *sui generis*, impervious, tough.

Scotland has been acclimatized to change by a history which has been a series of new beginnings. The initial union of tribes under Kenneth MacAlpin in 844 and then, with the addition of the Strathclyde Britons, under Malcolm Canmore in the eleventh century promoted an early sense of national identity which was strengthened by the wars of independence. Bannockburn was another beginning. In the sixteenth century the Reformation brought rejection of much of the past, melting significant edges of nationality in preparation for the first of the two most crucial new beginnings in 1603 when James VI of Scotland became James I of Great Britain, endowing British kingship with Arthurian status.[27] The second equally crucial new beginning came just over a century later in 1707 with what Lord Seafield allegedly called 'the end o' an auld sang'[28] when Scottish control energies absconded into the fundamentally English concept of Great Britain and the greater idea of empire. In 1707, with the union of the parliaments, Scotland embarked on a career as a colony in which life was increasingly determined by a 'signifying system' imposed by England. In the language used by theorists of Post-colonialism, England became the colonizing machine, Scotland the 'elided', colonized subject whose subjectivity is largely wished away.[29] Even today to be an urban, working-class Scottish writer is, apparently, to fear assimilation into a tradition of condescension or neglect, despite the successes of members of Philip Hobsbaum's writing groups in Glasgow, Anthony Burgess's admiration of Alasdair Gray's *Lanark*, Jeff Torrington's Whitbread Prize for *Swing Hammer Swing*, and *Sunday Times* praise for Edwin Morgan's translation of *Cyrano de Bergerac* into Glaswegian Scots. Reviewing James Kelman's essays in *Some Recent Attacks* (1992), Douglas Dunn sees in Kelman's opinions 'a heave from beneath, that is, an expression from a writer whose class and locale are traditionally disparaged by the literary mainstream'.[30]

There is no denying Scotland's collaboration in its own elision or the contributions made by opportunistic Scots to the building of empire. As Frederic Lindsay puts it:

> In the building of the empire which replaced the one muddled away with the American War of Independence, the Scots had played a disproportionate share. A quick conversion to the Anglican Church got them into the Indian Civil Service; they were missionaries in Africa and the traders who followed them; they instigated war with China in defence of the opium trade and sent the profits home to Dumfriesshire.[31]

With the disintegration of empire, what remains that may truly be called British except a passport? 'Britain', the weasel-word, has its contexts in officialese and on some, though by no means all, state occasions, but 'Britain' and 'British' too easily slip, slide and perish into 'England' and 'English'. A *Gramophone* review of recordings of Janáček's *Glagolitic Mass* includes the following:

> The *Glagolitic Mass* has been recorded by two British-based conductors, Mackerras and Rattle . . . and, of course, it is in no small part due to Mackerras that England has become, second only to his native land, a home for Janáček's music.[32]

The reviewer begins with good intentions – Mackerras and Rattle are 'British-based' – but when credit is due it is carried home to England and pop goes the weasel-word. For the Englishman Britain is England; for the Scot Britain is an English invention, a politically expedient fiction which, at best, protects Scotland from the bickering and callowness of its own nationalist politicians. Nevertheless, as Edwin Morgan puts it, 'the circle of empire is breaking, the satellites are escaping. If the 1990s are going to be the age of the periphery, Scotland too may take the plunge; not before time'.[33]

The most significant change in Scotland since 1707 is not to be found in the youth, adolescence or even, to speak optimistically, in the incipient maturity of the Scottish National Party. It is clearly not to be found in the fiasco of the 1979 referendum, more a Flodden than the second Bannockburn prophesied in 1724 by Allan Ramsay in 'The Vision'. Nor is it to be anticipated from the undertakings of an incoherent Labour Party flattened again by the Tory juggernaut in the 1992 British General Election. But it was there before the referendum in the impact of a poet's life and work. To changes in the status of the canon, in society and in the political map of the world, the great shifts in the contextual force-fields that have occurred over the last two decades, must be added changes in the Scottish literary sensibility which largely derive from Hugh MacDiarmid. He is the next and newest beginning. His pugnacious assertion of a Scottish literary character and his subversion of British (i.e. English) cultural hegemony were often cantankerous and splenetic, but his poems in Scots metabolized his idiosyncracies into the special authority of the language he revived to suit his and his country's needs. The resultant power became the prime cause of what is now called the Scottish Renaissance in literature of the twentieth century, a still under-valued composite *geist* made up of intensely individual writers who came to maturity during and after MacDiarmid, writers such as Robert Garioch, Norman MacCaig, Edwin Morgan, George Mackay Brown, Iain Crichton Smith and Sorley MacLean, a Gaelic poet imaginatively on the scale of Yeats.

The sense given by MacCaig's poetry of a conspicuously independent secular imagination negotiating the world on its own terms, Morgan's Glasgow-based internationality[34] and, among the profusion of newer talents, Alasdair Gray's anatomizing of Scottish culture represent a maturing beyond the inferiorist reflex and an end of paranoia. Politically Scotland may still be a colony, but in the arts of its letters it is no longer elided. The work of such writers is the final justification for a new assessment of Scotland's literary history and, thereby, a new definition of a Scottish canon. What Eliot calls the 'ideal order' of the existing monuments is modified by such work. With help from Watson and Wittig, David Daiches and David Craig, Duncan Glen, John MacQueen, Derick Thomson and others the modification should now be considered by that critical 'great love' whose perpetual duty is to keep us, as we evolve, consciously reconciled to our stones. It is by such a process that any periphery may become a centre. In 'The War with England' Hugh MacDiarmid exemplifies the right way to begin:

> I was better with the sounds of the sea
> Than with the voices of men
> And in desolate and desert places
> I found myself again
> For the whole of the world came from these
> And he who returns to the source
> May gauge the worth of the outcome
> And approve and perhaps reinforce
> Or disapprove and perhaps change its course.

University of Waikato

1 James Wood, 'Commentary: Derrida in Oxford', *TLS*, 3 April 1992, 13.

2 Lord Byron, *Selected Letters and Journals*, edited by Leslie A. Marchand (Cambridge, Mass., 1982), p. 100.

3 Samuel Johnson, *Rambler*, No 52, 15 September 1750, in *The Yale Edition of the Works of Samuel Johnson*, edited by W. J. Bate and Albrecht B. Strauss (New Haven and London, 1969), Vol. 3, p. 280.

4 Minnesota Humanities Commission, *Braided Lives* (St Paul, Minnesota, 1991), p. 9.

5 See T. S. Eliot, 'Tradition and the Individual Talent', in *Selected Essays* (London, 1927), p. 15.

6 *Braided Lives*, p. 273.

7 James Atlas, 'The Battle of the Books', *Dialogue*, 84 (February 1989), 24.

8 'Ferment in Education', *Dialogue*, 84 (February 1989), 21.

9 James Atlas, p. 29.

10 Ibid.

11 Alvin B. Kernan, 'The Death of Literature', *Princeton Alumni Weekly*, 22 January 1992, p. 13.

12 Pico Iyer, 'The Empire Writes Back', *Time*, 141, no. 6 (8 February 1993), 40.

13 George Steiner, *Real Presences* (London, 1989), p. 32.

14 See Robert Crawford, *Devolving English Literature* (Oxford, 1992).

15 The last five lines of MacDiarmid's poem are indebted to the third of E. E. Cummings's 'Seven Poems' in *&* *[AND]*, (1925), 'Spring is like a perhaps hand'. MacDiarmid's use of the borrowed lines is appreciative co-option rather than plagiarism: Cummings supplies a metaphor to help him develop a theme different from and larger than Cummings's own.

16 See Ian Carmichael, *Lismore in Alba* (Perth, 1947).

17 Burnett James, *The Music of Jean Sibelius* (London, 1983), p. 133.

18 For a scholarly and alarming discussion of the Scottish 'inferiorist reflex' see Craig Beveridge and Ronald Turnbull, *The Eclipse of Scottish Culture* (Edinburgh, 1989).

19 'You've Got the Wrong Man, Chum!', *Sunday Post*, 23 July 1978, p. 19.

20 Matthew Arnold, 'The Study of Poetry' in *Essays in Criticism*, Second Series, edited by S. R. Littlewood (London, 1938), pp. 26 and 29.

21 'Butcher Boiled His Friend', *Evening Times*, 28 May 1980, p. 1.

22 Marshall Walker, 'Scotch Drink, Scotch Manners and Scotch Religion', in *Living Out of London*, edited by Alan Ross (London, 1984), pp. 45–46.

23 Edward Said, *Musical Elaborations* (New York and London, 1991), p. 56.

24 Roderick Watson, *The Literature of Scotland* (Basingstoke, 1984).

25 David Cannadine, *The Decline and Fall of the British Aristocracy* (New Haven and London, 1990).

26 Edwin Morgan, 'Preface' to *Essays* (Cheadle, 1974), p. vii.

27 See Murray G. H. Pittock, *The Invention of Scotland: The Stuart myth and the Scottish identity, 1638 to the present* (London and New York, 1991), p. 4.

28 David Daiches, *Scotland and the Union* (London, 1977), p. 161.

29 David Trotter, 'Colonial Subjects', *Critical Quarterly*, vol. 32, no. 3 (1990), 3.

30 Douglas Dunn, 'I'm right and good, you're bad', *TLS*, 1 January 1993, p. 5.

31 Frederic Lindsay, 'A Union that Corrupts', *Scotland on Sunday*, 29 March 1992, p. 17.

32 John Warrack, *Gramophone*, vol. 69 (July 1991), 100. It is a fine irony that *Gramophone* was inaugurated by a Scottish music-lover, founded in 1923 by Sir Compton Mackenzie.

33 Edwin Morgan, 'Saturn and Other Rings', *Chapman*, 64 (Spring/Summer 1991), p. 10.

34 'Internationality' not 'internationalism', in deference to the distinction made by Tom Nairn in 'Internationalism: a critique', *The Bulletin of Scottish Politics*, vol. 1, no. 1 (Autumn, 1980), pp. 101–25. Note in particular: 'As for reality, all we need do is remember that the overwhelmingly dominant political by-product of modern internationality is nationalism. Not the logically prescribed common sense of internationalism, but the non-logical, untidy, refractory, disintegrative, particularistic truth of nation-states. Not swelling "higher unity" but "Balkanization", a world of spiky exceptions to what ought to have been the rule. The exceptions have become the rule'. (Ibid., p. 104). Morgan's themes and his affinities with the literatures of several languages connect his Scottishness to the concerns and idioms of many countries; but the 'political by-product' of his sympathies has recently been support for an independent Scotland.

Donald MacAulay

Canons, myths and cannon fodder

'Scotlands'. Is there within that plurality a Gaelic Scotland? If so how would we focus on it? How is it perceived? In what terms would we define it? Is there, indeed, a plurality of Gaelic Scotlands? What relationship do these have to non-Gaelic Scotland? What aspects of all this is it politically correct to talk about?

These questions are more than rhetorical. Long ago, for example, Scotland was ruled by a Gaelic leadership: Gaelic culture was the ascendant culture, the Gaelic language was the major language through which meaning in all prestigious domains (apart from the ritual dominance of Latin) was mediated. The very name 'Scotland' denoted Gaeldom. Its history is interesting: *Scotus* was the Latin word for 'Gael' or 'Irishman' (the Gaels, of course, came to Scotland from Ireland). *Scotia* developed as the distinctive Latin name of Scotland (as distinct from *Hibernia* for Ireland). 'Scotland' is, of course, patently an English word; the Gaels have always called Scotland *Alba*, an ancient name for mainland Britain. When Scotland had been officially Englished, and increasing areas of its land, and its developing towns in particular, were occupied by an English-speaking population, and that population and that English developed a distinctive identity of their own, those English speakers hijacked the term 'Scottish' to refer to their own speech. This was in contrast to earlier usage in English sources where men of 'Scottis' speech denoted Gaelic speakers, distinguishing them from men of 'Inglis' speech. Hence we get 'Scots', and 'Scottish' becomes a territorial rather than an ethnic term. To reinforce this transformation the Gaelic language came to be referred to in 'Inglis' as Irish: *'Irische'* or *'Earse'*. (Gaels in Scotland, as elsewhere, have always referred to their own language in their own language as 'Gàidhlig', or one of its co-variants.)

That was of course all a long, long time ago. But the purpose of this historical discursus, at the very beginning of what I have to say, is to establish the conviction that we do not get very far in understanding what Scotland is without reference to how it became what it is. The purpose, then, is not to blame the 'English' for displacing the 'Scots' or, indeed, to make a snide comment about how 'Scots' got its name. Scots are deeply concerned with their past, or what they conceive their past to be. It has to be conceded that that conception is often based on myth and hagiography, but that is not the point: the obsession is there and it persistently shapes the present. Furthermore, this is no new thing, and so we have a continual gradation of historical reshaping and reinforcement. 'Scotland' is the product of myth makers, who have drawn on different sources with different biases and different values. It is hard to find a consensus about reconstruction – even among contemporary historians, who seek to deconstruct the myths but often find it hard to play the bias.

And that problem is not a new one either. The purpose of the redefinition of linguistic and ethnic terms that we mentioned above was, clearly, at a particular historical juncture, to marginalise the Gaels, to define them as not properly belonging to the new, feudal Scotland. These redefinitions proved very useful in the conflicts of the seventeenth century aimed at making Scotland anew once more. The reference to 'the Irish language' is then repeated and contextualised in the following extract from the enactments of the Scottish Privy Council in 1616:

> Forsamekle as, the Kingis Majestie haveing a speciall care and regaird that the trew religioun be advanceit and establisheit in all the pairtis of this kingdome, and that all his Majesties subjectis, especiallie the youth, be exercised and trayned up in civilitie, godlines, knawledge, and learning, that the vulgar Inglishe toung be universallie plantit, and the Irish language, whilk is one of the cheif and principall causes of the continewance of barbaritie and incivilitie amongis the inhabitantis of the Isles and Hylandis, may be abolisheit and removit . . .

This is reinforced by another enactment. Clearly based on an act of Alexander IV in 1496, which laid down that all barons and freeholders should put their eldest sons and heirs to the schools 'quhill thai be competentlie foundit and ha perfyte Latyne', it required that the 'chiftanes and principal clannit man of the Ylles' should send their children being past nine years of age to the

> scollis in the Lawlandis to the effect that they may be instructit and trayned to wryte and reid and to speake Inglische; and that nane of their bairnes sall be served air unto them nor acknawlegeit nor received as tennentis to his Majestie unless they can wryte, reid, and speik Inglesche. (Register of the Privy Council, vol. 10, 773–81).

The policy that the barbarous tongue should be 'abolisheit and removit', at least from written discourse, in turn informed the attitude towards education and literacy in Gaelic Scotland for the next hundred and fifty years. This attitude defined out the Gaelic language as a tongue not fit for literacy, refusing to acknowledge that it had been the medium for some of the most sophisticated vernacular literature of the middle ages.

This seems an extraordinary attitude from a book-oriented elite which sought to provide access for all individuals to the literal Truth. To do them justice, they had another device for achieving this! All Gaelic speakers were to learn English, and the Scottish Society for the Propagation of Christian knowledge was contracted to effect that end. They strove valiantly at the task but they failed eventually. The New Testament in Gaelic was published in 1767 and the complete Bible was available by 1801. In the early nineteenth century the Gaelic Schools movement was supported by a number of bodies both religious and secular. However, the negative attitudes to Gaelic language and culture appear to have become endemic, and to be at best lying dormant in the greater Scottish body. This is clearly documented in such sources as the evidence given to the Nicolson Commission on Education in the Hebrides in the early eighteen sixties (Nicolson: 1866). This evidence shows that by then the attitude was affecting not only non-Gaels but was strongly expressed by some Gaels also, notably the Free Church minister of Harris who considered that it would be a decided benefit if Gaelic were to 'cease'. (Presumably, the church would then not have to waste its money training Gaelic-speaking ministers.) When the Education Act of 1872 was passed Gaelic was simply not mentioned. It was defined out by omission and the whole cycle had to begin again to gain a place for Gaelic in the education system.

This evidence of central disapproval undermined the confidence of Gaels in their own culture, which made the task of the bodies set up to resist it more difficult. Crises of confidence had, of course, been manifested at an earlier period, but the cultural strength of the Gaelic world had managed to cope with them. The earliest published anthology of vernacular Gaelic verse, collected by Raghnall Dubh in the island of Eigg and published in 1776 has an elegant English foreword which says that the collection is made before the Gaelic language disappears!

Raghnall's father Alasdair Mac Mhaighstir Alasdair, the greatest of the eighteenth-century Gaelic poets, published a collection of his verse in 1751 called *Ais-eiridh na Sean Chánoin Albannaich* (The Resurrection of the Ancient Scottish Tongue). The title poem makes exaggerated claims for the origin (the Garden of Eden) of the Gaelic language and for its superiority. Alasdair's book was reputedly burned by the public hangman in Edinburgh as seditious literature because of its advocacy of the Jacobite cause.

Mac Mhaigstir Alasdair is an interesting case of the ambivalence experienced by men of his class and origins in Gaelic Scotland in his time (and perhaps not only in his time). He was closely related to Clan Ranald, the continuing line of the Lords of the Isles. His father was an Episcopalian clergyman who lost his living through non-jurancy after the revolution of 1688. He was educated at Glasgow University and worked as a schoolmaster for the SSPCK. He was clearly entered into membership of the Scottish middle class. When Charles Stewart started his adventure, however, he welcomed him, changed his religion, and joined his army. As a poet he is also a prime documentary source of the effect that the Forty-five had on a certain class of Gael at least. He greeted Charles's arrival with rampant, joyous songs of welcome full of hope for the future:

> In the early morning as I awaken great is my eagerness and my rejoicing
> for I have heard that the Prince has come to the land of Clan Ranald.

When the adventure failed he composed a song in the form of an exchange between the prince and the Gaels which is full of the imagery of defeat:

> A thousand shrouds upon the world
> deceitful and dangerous are its ways
> the wheel of fortune has turned to our disadvantage

All Charlie's comforting promises are qualified:

> . . . we will gather our people together again
> when we can to battle.
> Put your trust . . . in the only One who will protect you . . .
> pray earnestly, tearfully, with fasting . . .

Hope and expectation are replaced by a posture of despair. These poems neatly document the emotional importance of the Forty-five: the raised hopes of traditional Gaels that it would bring a reversal in their cultural fortunes (however irrational that hope might have been), followed by the realisation that there simply was not going to be a Gaelic polity in Scotland. The Forty-five was followed by the *de iure* and *de facto* deconstruction of the remnants of traditional Gaelic society, and the consolidation of a new era. The tone of the dialogue poem we mentioned adumbrates a distinct and powerful strand of the verse that is to follow in the late eighteenth and nineteenth century. Predictions of doom are accompanied by their opposite: a verse in which the panegyric tradition, the proud boast of *ethnos* and kin, has largely become generalised and dissipated into a rhetoric of self-acclaim.

Versions of defensive rhetoric developed under threat at various crucial junctures in the history of the Gaels. Gaelic high-kingship in Scotland died out with the dynasty of Malcolm Canmore. Once feudalism was general and the Norse territories of the Hebrides were redeemed in the thirteenth century the Scottish central authority's drive towards one kingdom was *de iure* accomplished. *De facto*, however, large areas of the Gaelic west were non-consenting members, the most notable of these being the Lordship of the Isles, which, under the hegemony of Clan Donald survived through various vicissitudes to reach the peak of its power (at least territorially) in the early fifteenth century. By the end of the century, however, the Lord of the Isles had consented to being a mere peer of the realm of Scotland. This had a powerful symbolic significance for Gaels. The event was elegised by one of Clan Donald's classical bards: 'There is no joy without Clan Donald . . .' and the MacMhuirich bardic family followed the Clan Ranald branch, as the most authentic branch of the true blood, to Uist.

The demise of the Lordship of the Isles saw the end of the last semi-autonomous Gaelic polity, based perhaps on the traditional notion of regional kingship (the 'Lord of the Isles', *'Dominus Insularum'* in Latin, is referred to in Gaelic documents as *Rí Inssi Gall* 'King of the Hebrides'). The continuing ideal of a Gaelic political structure to represent the survival of Gaeldom remained in place after the Lordship's demise – its ghost one might say. This ghost sought resurrection in association with political and religious causes, and combinations of these, such as those embraced by Jacobitism. It was in such a context, following this ghost, that men such as Alasdair Mac Mhaighstir Alasdair risked all and came out in the Forty-five, and it was why eighteenth-century Gaelic poets of distinctly non-Catholic and distinctly non-Jamesite leanings and background composed 'Jacobite' songs. It is this also that made the defeat at Culloden assume such tragic proportions. The myth, with its deep roots in Gaeldom, had become defocussed and generalised.

After the Forty-five policies were applied which ensured that Scottish Gaeldom was brought within the economy of the realm and the legal and juridical rules which saw to it that that happened were put in place and enforced. There was a final end to the Chiefs' ability to have private armies. This disrupted the social order, with chieftains formerly seen as 'warlords' now transformed to being 'landlords'. The remnants of the traditional kin-based notion of society were eroded: the chief's relatives who had functioned in a quasi-military structure as officers of his army were now simply tenants, and when they could not provide their rent in money or kind they were no longer able to claim to supply it in service. So we get the first wave of emigration of Gaels to the New World.

We also get a new function for the military elements and traditions of Gaelic society. We must remember that the 'realm' was not now Scotland but Great Britain and that that realm was engaged in military ventures which demanded men with military skill. So Highland regiments were raised and officered (sometimes these officers had seen earlier service) and men recruited to them from the areas of origin of these officers. Thus both those officers, the middle class, and the men, the lower classes, found new identities for themselves, new loyalties to the British crown – to the King for his shilling. This loyalty became a potent, if again sometimes ambivalent, factor in the identity of the Gael, fostered and refocussed by the rhetoric that appealed to the traditional virtues of courage and obligation and applied to Britain's wars from the late seventeenth century onwards. This has resulted in strange ironies such as Allan of Kingsburgh, the husband of Flora MacDonald, who helped with Prince Charlie's escape after the Forty-five, having emigrated to the Carolinas, fighting as a half-pay officer in the British army on the side of the King in the American War of Independence; and after the American victory making plans to move with a group of Empire Loyalists from America to settle in Canada! Or take the case of the 'Highland' soldiers in Highland regiments fighting 'for King and country' in distant parts of the world while their families were being evicted and their homes burned.

How the loyalties of Gaels stood up to such vicissitudes is a matter of great interest and bears necessarily on how they saw the world and who they saw themselves to be. Alasdair Mac Mhaigstir Alasdair called the Gaelic language the 'ancient Scottish Language' not the 'ancient Gaelic Language' and that might lead us to think that by that time Gaels saw themselves as Scots rather than Gaels. However, it seems more likely that Alasdair's claim that Gaelic was the Scottish language was a function of the claim that Scotland was Gaelic in origin, and that he was claiming Scotland for the Gaels in much the same way as he claimed that Gaelic was the original language. It was a short step from there, perhaps, to the acquiring of British loyalties. These claims continued to be made in later times even when the evidence of the Gaels' relatively late arrival in Scotland from Ireland was generally accepted. Such claims of enhanced status tend to generate great power and to exert an influence on people's belief concerning identity which are entirely disproportionate to their credibility. They often arise in situations where status is depressed and when the cause or agent of suppression is particularly overbearing, and when the contrast of the present with the past is difficult to tolerate. One has only to examine the Ossianic controversy to see the different aspects of this phenomenon in action. James MacPherson on flimsy hearsay acquaintance with Gaelic heroic ballads invented his *Ossian*, giving the impression that it represented translations of authentic heroic verse. This was roundly denied on an even more flimsy basis by commentators who did not even know the Gaelic language. They denied that there were such things as ancient Gaelic manuscripts. This was met from the Gaelic world by a furious defence of MacPherson which went in some cases as far as to produce spurious Gaelic versions of his sources. This became a focus of identity and a yardstick for measuring loyalty. It is little wonder then that Gaelic identity has been a matter of debate and ambiguity.

In the traditional Gaelic community matters were simpler. A man was placed in terms of three parameters: *dùthchas*, which referred to his native place, *dualchas* which referred to his people or kin and *gnàthas* which referred to norms of personal behaviour; and the man was measured against expectations based on these norms. The first two, *dùthchas* and *dualchas*, were the traditional basis of identity and are very much recognised as such in the remnants of traditional society to this day: one belongs to a certain place and one belongs in the network of one's kin, just as surely – if in somewhat different terms – as was the case in the Middle Ages, where it is clearly delineated, for example, in panegyric verse. There it comprises a fundamental feature of the mirror of perfection held up to the chief by his poet. In the middle of the twentieth century, when a young man left home to seek his fortune in other parts, one overriding injunction was given to him – whatever other Polonian or Paulian advice might be tendered – *Cuimhnich cò thu*! 'Remember who you are'. In the context, that was neither vacuous nor arrogant. It points to the nexus of community and family that defined the individual, and to the advantages and obligations that are understood to flow therefrom.

One of the results of the attempt to bring the Highlands into the general British economy in the late eighteenth and nineteenth century was the development first of all of large areas of sheepruns and when that proved uneconomic the diversification in the middle of the nineteenth century into sporting estates. Both of these ventures resulted in population displacement and large-scale emigration, most of it to Scottish cities. This brought with it its own set of identity problems, the response to which bears out the kinds of understanding of the nature of identity that we have been talking about.

One finds in all cities where Gaels settled a Gaelic Society – a superstructure which serves as a focus for retaining a Gaelic identity, where Gaelic related social and cultural activities were pursued. This is, of course, not very different from the behaviour of other emigré groups. There are, however, peculiar aspects to the Gaelic diaspora, which may be illustrated by the Glasgow experience, for example. To this city came Gaels in considerable numbers from most parts of Gaeldom, and here they proceeded to establish area-based societies, named after the places of origin of the members in the Islands and on the Scottish mainland. Some of these societies, such as the 'Lewis and Harris' and the 'Skye' associations, for example, came to occupy a crucial place in the lives of members, offering them an identity and a social place in their new environment and indeed eventually offering them a distinct place in the social life of the city if they became leaders in their society. These societies and associations were, of course, structures of the city and it was from that that they derived their social status. Members, however, tended to see them as a continuation of their home communities; and thus they supported the city Gaels' duality of identity. Gaels could come to Glasgow as young people, spend their whole lives in Govan and still, when asked in old age where they came from, they would say they came from Uist, or from Sutherland, or whatever their place of origin was. Furthermore, their children born and brought up in Glasgow, and entirely accultured Glaswegians in speech and habit, were likely to say the same; and their grandchildren also, even if they had visited the ancestral place only once or twice (or indeed not at all) would, provided they had kept in touch with the local organisation, cite the place as 'where they came from'. This, of course, complicated the definition of 'Gael'. These generations would be 'Gaelic' in quite different senses.

The matter of *dualchas* or kinship was exploited in a similar way by the development of 'Clan Societies'. In this case people with the same surname are eligible to be members, one is tempted to say irrespective of their origins. Clanship in this sense is entirely different, of course, from the traditional Gaelic *cinneadh* which was based on a four-generation kingroup, and from the looser *clann*, 'descendants', which was based on descent from one ancestor. It has, however, got great advantages of visibility: each Clan has its own tartan, often two, 'dress' and 'hunting', which neatly brackets the context in which they flourish. It works wonders for the souvenir business. One is not surprised that its true potential was discovered by a German tourist and exploited by a Lowland entrepreneurial laird!

It must be said that the status won by both Gaelic societies and tartanry brought some respectability to Gaels in the eyes of outsiders, though, in general, the terms of derogation remained in place! (See under 'Hieland', 'teuchter' in The Scots Thesaurus §15.2.2., for example.) It must also be said that attitudes derived from city Gaeldom filtered back to the homeland, and that these were a potent force in the transformation of Gaelic traditional culture. Migration was not always for life; indeed, the commonest kind was seasonal or was entered into for fixed terms, and it was normal for emigrants to maintain strong home contacts and to make regular visits to their home community. The question of Gaelic identity, then, presents problems. The answer to 'Who is a Gael?' depends on when you ask it and of whom you ask it – and, indeed, in what language you ask it! If you ask it of a non-Gaelic-speaking Scot, the most likely answer you get is 'a Hielander' (see above!) – they have problems with the difference between 'What is a Gael?' and 'Who is a Gael?': a Gael is, generally, someone who lives vaguely north by west. If you ask a Gaelic-speaking Scot who has learned Gaelic as a non-native language (and perhaps some politically correct attitudes at the same time) they are likely to say 'Some one from Gaeldom' (excluding themselves, even if they are Gaelic speakers). If you ask a native community Gaelic-speaker, in English (they are all bilingual), they are likely to say 'Someone from the

Gaeltachd', and get into trouble both with narrower definitions – in terms of language, for example; and broader definitions – in terms of parental origins, for example. If you ask a traditional Gaelic-speaker in Gaelic, there does not appear to be such indecisiveness: *'Duine aig a bheil Gàidhlig bho dhùthchas'* 'A native speaker of Gaelic' (or words to that effect) will be your most likely answer. Language will be the primary criterion. Traditionally the term *Gaidheal* contrasted with *Gall, Gaidheal* denoting a member of the Gaelic ethnolinguistic community and *Gall* denoting someone who was not: a foreigner. The word *Gall* has tended to be used in more recent times to mean a Scot who is not a member of the Gaelic ethnolinguistic community; other nationalities are specifically named, e.g., *Sasannach*, 'Englishman', *Frangach*, 'Frenchman', and so forth.

At the present time, of course, an added complexity has arisen which separates out the ethnic and the linguistic components. Many people have learned the Gaelic language who do not belong to the Gaelic community. They pass the linguistic test, however. On the other hand many young members of the Gaelic community fail to learn the Gaelic language, and so they do not fulfil the linguistic criterion. And, meantime, we have traditional speakers. We need to develop terms which will, neutrally, differentiate among them. As we have said Gaelic identity is a complex question.

Nevertheless there is, I think, a 'Gaelic Scotland'. The problem is that it is multifaceted and discontinuous, consisting of networks as well as communities. The most agreed criterion for Gaelicness and the most marked (though not entirely clear cut, as we have said) is the native-speaker one. Overwhelmingly, Gaelic speakers have been (and are) native speakers: they belong to an ethnolinguistic community. If we look at their numbers and the area of their geographical distribution we find that both of these, in the period that census figures have been available to us, have inexorably decreased.

The table shows us the population decline. The earliest numbers are based on estimates. The first census, in 1881, shows numbers of monoglot Gaelic speakers, the first count of Gaelic and English bilinguals being in 1891. From then until 1981, when no data on Gaelic-only speakers was collected for the first time (the number of monoglots being deemed negligible), figures for both Gaelic monoglots and Gaelic-English bilinguals are given. The most striking feature of the table is the decline in speakers of Gaelic only from around 300,000 in 1800 to virtually none in 1980. This, of course, reflects the negative continuing marginalisation of the Gaelic language in a large numbers of domains, particularly education, and the positive opening out of the contiguous world of English to Gaelic speakers. This decline is paralleled, but less drastically, by the decline of speakers of Gaelic and English. The figures for 1971 show an apparent reversal of this pattern with 88,892 speakers as against 80,978 in 1961 (counting both monoglots and bilinguals).

Gaelic Speakers in Scotland, c.1755–1991

Source	Scottish Population	Speakers of Gaelic only	Speakers of Gaelic and English	Speakers of Gaelic and English as % of population
c.1755	1,265,380	289,798		
c.1800	1,608,420	297,823		
1881	3,735,573	231,594		
1891	4,025,647	43,738	210,677	5.2
1901	4,472,103	28,106	202,700	4.5
1911	4,760,904	18,400	183,998	3.9
1921	4,573,471	9,829	148,950	3.3
1931	4,588,909	6,716	129,419	2.8
1951	5,096,415	2,178	93,269	1.8
1961	5,179,344	974	80,004	1.5
1971	5,228,965	477	88,415	1.7
1981	5,035,315	—	82,620	1.6
1991			c.65,000	

This reversal derives from a change in attitude to Gaelic census reporting as much as anything else. This attitude is reflected in and reflects the fight for recognition which went on during the 1970s coinciding (serendipitously) with the establishment of *Comhairle nan Eilean* and foreshadowing the drive towards the establishment of other Gaelic-promoting structures. The reversal continues in the data for 1981 which in answer to a reformed designation 'speaks, reads or writes Gaelic' show 82,620 Gaelic users. The figure for 1991 of around 65,000 shows that there is an underlying trend of decline. The official statistics for 1991 have not yet been published in detail.

The area of Scotland in which majority traditional Gaelic-speaking communities have survived is now confined to the Islands. The situation, however, is not, perhaps, as bad as it seems. As older traditional speakers decline in number, new initiatives to produce learner Gaelic speakers, both adults and children, have brought encouraging results. Structures have been put in place such as *Comann an Luchd Ionnsachaidh* (The Gaelic Learners Association) and *Comhairle nan Sgoiltean Araich* (The Gaelic Nursery Schools) movement. School education facilities are being set up, with learners classes and Gaelic medium units in schools in Gaelic areas and in cities where there is a demand for them from the parents of children wishing them to become fluent in the language and to use it in the process of education. There has, indeed, been a gradual 'Gaelicisation' of education discernible since the 1960s, which has gone hand in hand with the gradual recognition of the status of Gaelic. Both developments have been slow moving, and their history complicated. (There is a useful overview in Kenneth MacKinnon's *Gaelic – A Past and Future Prospect (1991), Section II)*.

The strongest recent impetus to change in the status of the Gaelic world was probably given by the belated recognition by the Highlands and Islands Development Board of its social remit. This derived from its promotion of community co-operatives in the Gaelic area and culminated in its setting up a Gaelic committee which in turn commissioned a report on the economic, cultural and social context of the language which was published in 1982 with the title *Cor na Gàidhlig*. The report identified a number of lacks in education and the communicative arts and called for institutional remedies for the obvious fragmentation of effort to be seen in the Gaelic world; it called for the Gaelic language to be seen in the context of community and economic development and in a national rather than a narrow context.

Many of the recommendations of the report have been accepted. In 1984 the HIDB established a Gaelic development programme and amongst other initiatives a Gaelic committee *Comann na Gàidhlig* (CnaG) was set up, with substantial funding, to oversee developments. It is no coincidence that the Montgomery Committee on Island administration was published in the same year, nor should we forget the Arfé resolutions of 1981 and 1983 on the rights of minority languages, the former of which led directly to the establishment in 1982 of the European Bureau for Lesser-Used Languages. Pressures were coming to bear on the British Government which ensured that to some degree at least the transformations that were taking place in Gaelic Scotland, and which had positive potential, gained a modicum of support. One of the areas in which potential has been fulfilled is that of the media of radio and television. The Government was not persuaded by CnaG (any more that former Governments had been persuaded by earlier lobbyists) that it should adopt a national policy for Gaelic, to provide a context for the Gaelic and bilingual policies of local authorities, but CnaG's arguments for the development of television were apparently more persuasive. The result was that at the end of 1989 the Government announced the setting up of a Gaelic Television Fund of £8m to increase output of Gaelic television to about 200 hours per year. This fund has since been increased to the best part of £10m.

As one might expect, this largesse has occasioned some debate, motivated by a range of different considerations. There have to be two (in particular) worries voiced in the Gaelic community. Firstly, many people think the Government has its priorities wrong: that if it had £10m to give it should have given it to a project which would show more permanent results for the common good than television programmes are likely to. This is a point of view; it is acceptable provided it remains a criticism of Government and does not lead to animus against the beneficiaries of the Fund, or their product, which must be judged on its own terms. The other worry has been that the products themselves might be unworthy. This is a genuine worry, for the Gaelic community is not in a position to bear negative exploitation. Its very survival is too finely balanced. Up to now, the worry (if not entirely dispelled) seems to have been comparatively needless. The programmes produced under the aegis of the Fund represent a reasonable spread of topics: historical exposition, language teaching, and entertainment – ranging from game show to soap. The quality, it must be said, is mixed; but at its best it compares favourable with English-language correlates, and it has to be borne in mind that there has not been a sufficient period of time to provide adequate training, not to mention experiential consolidation. Audience reaction, after an initial period of some shock among traditionalists, seems to have come around to being generally favourable. People look forward to the next programme in a series and lend themselves to the experiences being presented. Certainly, Gaelic culture will never be the same again . . .

The reactions from outside the Gaelic community have been interesting. Some have been supportive, some have been pragmatic, waiting to judge the quality, and the accessibility for them, of the product. Some have been covertly and some openly hostile. It is undeniably the case that there remains in the wider Scottish community an endemic anti-Gaelic bias, which tends to manifest itself whenever Gaelic matters acquire a high profile of a positive kind. And what better to activate it than the 'gift' of £8m of Government money! Envy has been a conspicuous motivation for negative comment on the Fund from those outside the Gaelic community and from some who would claim to belong to it (without the language, usually). 'Why should that sort of money be spent on a dying/dead language?' is a frequent question. Usually the question is a rhetorical one: the questioner, of course, knows the appropriate answer. The grant for Gaelic is often cited in the context of the lack of support for Scots, as if the latter was precluded, somehow or other, by the former. One Scottish newspaper has run what amounts to an anti-Gae-lic campaign hung on this peg. The announcement that the Scottish soap *Take the High Road* was to be axed recently was the occasion for a radio 'live' phone-in show to be devoted to that topic, quite rightly. What seemed to be not so relevant was that this was combined with questions on the participants' attitudes to Gaelic programmes on television, as if the threat to *Take the High Road* and the presence of Gaelic television programmes were directly related to one another, when, in fact, they are quite unrelated. This bias is a taboo topic in the opinion of some – in the interests of Scottish solidarity. But it needs to be discussed openly. Clearly, keeping quiet about it has not made it go away. It needs to be said that history shows us that the specific enemies of Gaelic culture have always been in Scotland, not in England or in some other vague and distant place, and that they are still there. Otherwise we will be unable to engage in rational dialogue about the matter, and the bias we have mentioned will remain without definition or critical contextualisation, to be exploited by any vested interest that wishes to take advantage of it. Perhaps the advocates of silence should consider that politicians, professional and amateur, know all about the divisiveness of the politics of envy.

Gaelic culture and its context have in the present century undergone profound transformations. The economy, for example, certainly in the crofting area, has seen a change from what was largely a subsistence economy in which crofters produce the bulk of their own food to a pretty well complete market economy dependent on a viable money income. This has resulted in radically altered patterns of life, work and leisure. It has for example completed the move away from mutual dependence to the self-sufficient single family unit which the individualisation of crofts set up the model for at the beginning of the nineteenth century. Crofters, however, tended to retain their traditional mutual help work patterns and their communal patterns of cultural life. These patterns died hard, but were helped on their way conspicuously by the two World Wars, which were profound watersheds in Gaelic life. The most important factor was probably the way in which their war experiences opened out the world to those who served in them. They were able to exploit the outside world and many were eager to avail themselves of the opportunities that it afforded. This, together with lack of opportunity at home, resulted in heavy out-migration.

During the 1914–18 period crucial aspects of the subsistence economy, which entailed intensive cultivation, could not be sustained, and staple elements of food had to be bought in and money for this had to be earned, and with local employment scarce after the war, seasonal migration, a continuing pattern, was intensified and often replaced by out-migration of both men and women to jobs in the cities of Britain and America. Local communities began to be emptied of their youth. This continued in the thirties and when the 1939–45 war came the community was once more denuded of young men – the large majority were naval or army reservists – and on this occasion many young women departed also. After the war, after a brief respite for recuperation, the out-migration pattern was repeated. The result was that crofts in many areas became, at best, bases from which families could make a living at non-crofting jobs, and agriculture largely became narrowed to sheep rearing. At worst, crofts became the last havens of the elderly as they waited for death or the old peoples home. Even in those areas that kept a viable population the traditional cultural patterns changed radically. This became the era of the wireless and then the television, the era when thatched houses finally gave way to slated houses, wells to tap water, outside 'toilets' to inside toilets, the fire in the middle of the floor to the stove, to the cooker, to the microwave. It is the age when almost as many

Gaels live outside the Gaelic community, in networks or as individuals, as live within it. This has resulted in a society where there is a very marked cultural differentiation between the older age groups, who have very well marked cultural identities and cultural self-definition, to the youth who, apart from language (where that is maintained), often do not make any significant distinction in culture between themselves and their non-Gaelic contemporaries. And indeed they do embrace many of the same cultural norms. We said of city Gaels, above, that each of three generations could be 'Gaels' in a different sense. The same is coming to be increasingly true of three generation families in the Gaeltachd.

Gaelic literature in the twentieth century reflects the cultural norms and changes we have been discussing. Before the Second World War Gaelic literature was essentially traditional in form. There had been attempts to develop the short story along contemporary lines during the first decade of the twentieth century and that was followed by attempts to develop the Gaelic novel, but both of these lost steam and the second in particular was not successful. These efforts were conducted in the Gaelic emigré community, in the city, where there was access to printing presses and models for 'literature' and publication. Although, in the nineteenth century, traditions of Gaelic literacy were being revived, the meaningful literature of the Gaelic community was largely oral – traditional verse, folktale and anecdote, and lore, traditional and biblical in origin. Oral literature, whether entertainment or other, does not have to be oral in origin, of course. Memory, in an oral culture, is strongly developed and a story heard read is as easy to commit to memory as one heard recited. The Gaelic literary repertoire was thus fed from many sources.

It is conspicuously the case that the oral tale tradition did not feed fruitfully into the literary prose tale tradition, probably because literary prose fiction requires particular social conditions to flourish and these conditions were not unambiguously fulfilled in the Gaelic context until the fifties. By that time the world had changed sufficiently for writers, of the short story in particular, to emerge who were not inhibited by the expectations of earlier efforts in the genre in Gaelic. Some, indeed, did continue to model their work on that of earlier writers, to choose similar themes or to use their prolix and often register-deaf modes of writing, whilst being apparently innovatory in their choice of subjects, with science fiction providing the most common innovatory element. Some of these stories are of considerable interest as fiction, but more often their fascination lies in the light they shed on the writers' perception of their 'world' and how their creations relate to the world of their social experience in the Gaelic context – or indeed how, through lack of irony in their narrative for example, they seem set on not articulating that world. The real advances are made, however, by those writers whose work looks beyond earlier Gaelic models, learn from the masters of fiction, and develop their own individual visions and skills.

The advances are, basically, twofold: the development of a plain, overt style of exposition to express complex characterisation and deal with complex ideas; and the development of flexible and variant language techniques to explore the heart of the Gaelic community. These approaches require different skills. What their successful practitioners have in common is a clear vision of their goals. We see them deployed first of all in the short story. This has now, after a considerable period, led to their development in the novella or the short novel.

The conspicuous practioner of the former technique, and the most productive of Gaelic prose writers, is Iain Mac a' Ghobhainn (Iain Crichton Smith). The range of his Gaelic fiction is similar to that of his English work though the extent is not as great. In his earlier short stories we see him dealing with 'epiphanies', confrontations, psychological dilemmas, the loneliness of the individual, cultural displacement, masks and identity, individual responsibility. These same themes are explored in his Gaelic novels, *An t-Aonaran* (The Loner) and *Na Speuclairean Dubha* (The Dark Glasses). In the former he explores the dilemnas of the members of a village community through the device of introducing the 'Aonaran' who is unknown to them all, has no history, lives by himself, virtually independent of social contact. He acts as a catalyst that activates debates within and between the villagers which reveal their inner lives to us. *Na Speuclairean Dubha* has as its hero-narrator a detective whose inner life and problems of identity and responsibility and vulnerability are explored. Both of these novels are sophisticated, highly developed, and humane achievements, and bear centrally – but of course not exclusively – on the dilemmas of the Gaelic world.

The second kind of advance is associated with the short stories of Iain Moireach as seen in his important collection *An Aghaidh Choimheach* (The Mask). This collection explores aspects of the Gaelic community or of the individual in the context of the community, usually by letting the social group speak for itself, by utilising a (highly selective) social realism, to depict social initiation, rites of passage and the richness and bathos of social interaction. This style, or at least styles related to it, is used in the development of longer fiction by Tormod Caimbeul in *Deireadh an Fhoghair* (The End of Autumn) in which the last survivors in a village, in their old age, ruminate on their lives as they are and as they have been. Alasdair Caimbeul's *Am Fear Meadhanach* (The Middle One [also: The Middling One]) tells anecdotally, with irony and humour and in his own words, the life of Murchadh, who, after a lifetime of schoolteaching, comes back to his native Lewis to die and to relive his life in memory. These novels are rooted in the Gaelic community, deal with Gaels in their eccentric worlds and use a language which is vital and bears witness at least to survival. As well as those writers we have mentioned there have been a number of other excellent writers, particularly of the short story.

Gaelic poetry in the twentieth century has inherited a much more complex tradition than the prose. Up to the late thirties all Gaelic verse – apart from some rare pieces that stood apart – was traditional in form and traditional in theme. Indeed this kind of verse continues to be composed until the present time, although it is now greatly reduced in its volume and in its range and power. Gaelic verse in the nineteenth century, and in the early twentieth century also, tends to get a bad press. Some of this is, no doubt, deserved. We said above that in the late eighteenth century poetry began to reflect the lack of self-confidence of Gaels in their culture and in their future, and that that situation in turn generated an unrealistic rhetoric of self-acclaim. Poetry of nostalgia, longing for 'home' and for the past, typified the verse of the city Gaels in the nineteenth century. Such poetry became a fashion which was very difficult to resist; it became part of the cement which was required to provide the exile Gaels, who were its primary audience, with a social identity; it was the common coinage of their culture. In short it became 'politically correct', and its modes and language became stereotyped and wooden.

Having said that, two other things need to be said. Firstly, not all emigré verse falls to be castigated for these faults. There were practitioners who did not follow the prevailing tendency, or who sometimes wrote with an eye on their audience and sometimes did not; they belonged, after all, to two communities, their home community and the city community into which they had moved, and they had models of poetry from both and emotional bonds and allegiances in both. There were also those whose natural genius and skills allowed them to surmount artificial boundaries. The second point that requires to be made is that throughout this period traditional 'unreconstructed' poets continued to compose their verse and to fulfil their traditional roles in the Gaelic community as these roles had been historically defined, and revised, from antiquity. As far back as evidence about poets goes in the Celtic world they had crucial social roles in their society. In early times they belonged to a special learned class whose duties had a sacred sanction. In historical times in Gaelic society one of their prime duties was to hold up the mirror of perfection to their aristocratic patrons. They praised them, saying that they were of true descent and the acme of the virtues of courage, wisdom and generosity; and if they fell short of these expectations, then the whole natural order would fail, the land would be blighted of crops, cattle would be barren, and the weather would be bad; and the patrons would be without honour or fame. After these beliefs had been abandoned, or at best became formalised and symbolic, poets retained aspects of their former calling. They were the social commentators of their society, passing 'communal' judgement on events in it and in the world about it. It is interesting for us to see the religious poet Dughall Bochanan in Perthshire in the eighteenth century remaking the 'warrior' as the Christian warrior, quite explicitly utilizing the form and language of traditional panegyric, and in the same century to see Rob Donn in Sutherland doing the same for the social virtues in his eulogies on his MacKay patrons. Christian and humane virtues were again invoked in the nineteenth century in the poetry of the land conflicts. This tradition survived in a pretty robust form into the middle of the twentieth century, by which time the poetry of praise was thin on the ground except in religious panegyric and the occasional elegy; but the poetry of social criticism on a community basis was common enough, often couched in humorous terms. The characteristics of this poetry were that it was well-wrought technically and was rich in verbal wit and allusion.

Modern Gaelic poetry began and developed in a situation of contact with other traditions, notably the developing English poetic tradition, and in reaction to certain aspects of the Gaelic tradition which were felt to be no longer capable of articulating the meanings of evolving Gaelic society. The negative reaction was mostly against the poetry of nostalgia which was seen as expressing the negative and weak aspects of the Gaelic world and failing to project a true image of it. The reaction was not against the continuing panegyric tradition as it was to be found in the traditional community, though that was seen also, and properly so, as having become diminished and attenuated, and often having primarily local reference.

The first collection of Gaelic poems in the modern idiom was Somhairle MacGill-Eain's *Dàin do Eimhir agus Dàin Eile* (1943). It was at the time regarded as being very avant-garde, and it was indeed truly innovative. On maturer reflection it is, I think, to be considered as the vital link between the traditional verse and the new. The fact that it retains much of the strengths of the tradition, indeed is a constant allusion to it, and at the same time uses the material in a strikingly new way, is the main reason for the impact that the volume made on its readers. As well as the panegyric tradition there has been in Gaelic verse a strongly-defined lyric tradition in which the love poem has been the major species. *Dàin do Eimhir* may be said to be about love on the one hand and, on the other, about obligation, which is the crucial theme of the panegyric tradition. Somhairle MacGhill-Eain, then, brings powers of passion and intellect to bear on two major themes of Gaelic poetry and investigates the tensions between them in a cultural and political nexus. It was without a doubt a poetry for the times.

The next collection of modern Gaelic verse had largely different concerns and showed no discernible influence from *Dàin do Eimhir*. This was *Fuaran Slèibh* (1947) by Deòrsa Cambeul Hay, whose interests were in nature, nationalism and tradition at that stage of his career. *An Dealbh Briste*, however, by Ruaraidh MacThòmais, published 1951, does show such influence along with a distinctive voice of his own. This voice, articulating concerns about Gaelic and Scottish identity and society, has become one of the most distinguished and influential in modern Gaelic verse.

Those three – MacGhill-Eain, Hay and MacThòmais – have achieved major poetic stature in Gaelic and Scottish literature. The status of their work together with that of Iain Mac a'Ghobhainn was given recognition by its publication, together with English translation which opened their work to a wider audience, in the anthology *Nua-Bhàrdachd Ghàidhlig* (1976). Since that time Mac a'Ghobhainn has published a number of volumes of excellent verse. MacGhill-Eain and MacThòmais have published collected editions (again with translations) *O Choille gu Bearradh* (From Wood to Ridge) (1989) and *A' Creachadh na Clarsaich* (Plundering the Harp) (1982) respectively. A collection of Hay's verse in Gaelic and Scots is in preparation. MacThòmais has recently published a new collection *Smeur an Dòchais* (The Bramble of Hope) (1991). These works have become the canon of modern Gaelic verse.

In the meantime a new generation of Gaelic poets has arrived, most of whom have published collections of their verse. An anthology of it, with English translations, has recently been published, edited by one of the contributors, Christopher Whyte: *An Aghaidh na Sìorraidheachd* (In the Face of Eternity) (1991). The poetry shows considerable continuity in theme and style from the older generation, in some cases quite close imitation, and differing degrees of empathy with the Gaelic tradition (apart from one contributor who does not seem to exhibit these connections). The group covers a considerable age range, four born in the 1940s, three in the 1950s, and one in the 1960s, and their work shows in general, as well as the Gaelic influence we have mentioned, an awareness of the poetic movements of their formative years in the wider context. As far as quality is concerned it compares very favourably with that seen in contemporary English anthologies.

There is one feature of this group which, if not new, has hitherto been very rare in Gaelic poetry. Of the eight poets featured three are not native speakers of Gaelic. (Hay also learned the language.) This repeats a pattern well established in Ireland, and is a sign of the times. Traditional poets learned their craft in the context of an oral tradition; some were only marginally literate even in the twentieth century. With the development of literacy that changed, of course, but even those who were highly literate learned the skills of their craft largely in an oral context. What literacy and publication did was to provide a larger context of information about the tradition and exemplification of it beyond what was available locally and through traditional channels. These examples often fed into and enriched the oral tradition.

Modern poetry resides primarily in the written medium (however much it is influenced by the oral). In this way it has altered the nature of Gaelic literature and hence the definition of Gaelic culture. This, and its introduction of exotic elements, and forms such as *vers libre*, are its crucial cultural contribution. It has made the Gaelic world conscious of the power of the written medium and has thus pointed up the importance of publishing, the remarkable development of which, with the establishment of *Gairm* Publications at the beginning of the fifties, followed by the Gaelic Books Council in 1968 and *Acair* plc at the end of 1978, has wrought an important cultural transformation.

The publication of translations along with the verse has allowed access to it for non-Gaelic speakers and there is no doubt that, as a result, the status of Gaelic poets and poetry has risen in the eyes of non-Gaels. Gaelic literature has become a more acceptable commodity for main-stream publishers and literary entrepreneurs, and indeed for all who see themselves as connoisseurs of literary forms. And this has enhanced the status of Gaelic culture, which is a highly desirable development.

It is not, however, without its cultural dangers. There is, for example, an assumption articulated (and defended) by some people in the literary establishment, and elsewhere, in Scotland that the translation can somehow be an adequate substitute for the original – not the best available to one because one does not know the language of the original and so can have no direct access to it, which is a reasonable point of view, but that the translation itself is somehow equally valued with the original. This assumption does not, of course, bear sensible examination. The words in a language carry with them their histories and connotations. Gaelic poetic vocabulary has undergone a series of contextual rehabilitations over hundreds of generations and Gaelic poetic discourse exploits these polysemies. They are not amenable to word for word, or line by line, translation. This problem is not confined to artefacts in the Gaelic language alone, of course, but Gaelic is a particularly striking case.

All Gaelic speakers are bilingual, as we have said above. They have different degrees of bilingual competence and preference. Reading the latest (bilingual) anthology *An Aghaidh na Sìorraidheachd* I was concerned to find that with some poems I felt unable to determine, from reading them, which was the translation and which the original. I found myself contemplating the notion of perfectly balanced bilingualism – but I fear that that will not bear scrutiny either. For many reasons – lack of personnel, difficulty with consensus (the Gaelic world is factional rather than consensual), dissipation of effort, problems with models, it has proved difficult to develop a vigorous, flexible and coherent body of indigenous criticism. Without it, considering the problems of knowledge and understanding which Gaelic culture faces, there is a danger that it will finally, for all the admirable fiscal and political structures put in place, be defined out – translated into non-distinctiveness. Which raises an interesting question for all 'Scotlands' to ponder. 🍎

University of Glasgow

Caimbeul, A, *Am Fear Meadhanach*, Conon Bridge, Druim Fraoich, 1992.

Caimbeul, T, *Deireadh an Fhoghair*, Edinburgh, Chambers, 1979.

Chapman, M, *The Gaelic Vision in Scottish Culture*, London, Croom Helm, 1979.

Hay, G C, *Fuaran Slèibh*, Glasgow, William MacLellan, 1947.

Mac a'Ghobhainn, I, *An t-Aonaran*, Glasgow, University of Glasgow Department of Celtic, 1976.

Mac a'Ghobhainn, I, *An t-Eilean agus an Cànan*, Glasgow, University of Glasgow Department of Celtic, 1987.

Mac a'Ghobhainn, I, *Na Speuclairean Dubha*, Glasgow, Gairm, 1989.

MacAmhlaigh, D, *Nua-Bhàrdachd Ghàidhlig: Modern Scottish Gaelic Poems*, Edinburgh, Southside, 1976; Canongate, 1987.

MacGhill-Eain, S, *Dàin do Eimhir agus Dàin Eile*, Glasgow, William McLellan, 1943.

MacGhill-Eain, S, *O Choille gu Bearradh*, Manchester, Carcanet, 1979.

MacKinnon, K M, *Gaelic – A Past and Future Prospect*, Edinburgh, Saltire, 1991.

MacThòmais, R, *An Dealbh Briste*, Edinburgh, Serif Books, 1951.

MacThòmais, R, *A'Creachadh na Clarsaich*, Edinburgh, MacDonald, 1982.

MacThòmais, R, *Smeur an Dòchais*, Edinburgh, Canongate, 1991.

Moireach, I, *An Aghaidh Choimheach*, Glasgow, Gairm, 1973; reprinted 1993.

Nicolson, A, *Education Scotland Commission, Report on the State of Education in the Hebrides by Alexander Nicolson*, Parliamentary Papers., 1867.

Smith, I C, *Towards the Human*, Edinburgh, MacDonald Publishers, 1986.

Whyte, C, *An Aghaidh na Sìorraidheachd*, Edinburgh, Polygon, 1991.

ROBERT CRAWFORD

Bakhtin and Scotlands

Each morning when I walk to work along North Street, St Andrews, I pass a
building that bears a small blue plaque:

JAMES CRICHTON, 1560–1582
STYLED 'THE ADMIRABLE'

BORN AT ELIOCK IN DUMFRIES, HE LIVED HERE WHILE A
STUDENT. A GREAT PERSONALITY OF HIS TIME, LEARNED IN
PHILOSOPHY AND SCIENCE, FLUENT IN GREEK, LATIN, ARABIC,
HEBREW, FRENCH, ITALIAN, SPANISH AND ENGLISH, EXPERT
HORSEMAN, SWORDSMAN AND MUSICIAN, IN A DISPUTATION IN
PARIS IN 1580 HE DEFEATED THE FRENCH SCHOLARS, AND WAS
CALLED 'ADMIRABLE'. SIMILAR SUCCESS IN ITALY LED THE DUKE
OF MANTUA TO APPOINT HIM TO HIS COUNCIL. THIS ANGERED
THE PRINCE, HIS SON, WHO FEARED FOR HIS OWN POSITION.
LATE ONE NIGHT HE MET CRICHTON AND STABBED HIM TO
DEATH. HE IS BURIED IN THE CHURCH OF SAN SIMONE IN
MANTUA, AND HE IS IMMORTALISED IN BARRIE'S PLAY 'THE
ADMIRABLE CRICHTON'.

The plaque translates the building into multiple contexts, relating it, albeit
tangentially, to Scottish intellectual history, French intellectual history, Italian political history, and (implicitly) to the idea of a heteroglot European
community in which Scotland can be a player. More immediately, the plaque
marks the building as a site of intersection between several canons, most
notably the historical and the literary. Since few sixteenth-century Scottish
student residences survive, this house, part of the architectural canon of
'listed buildings', and enhanced by its link with a particular notable individual, seems securely canonical, a status likely to guarantee its continued
existence. The plaque also relates the building to the literary canon, to a play

by Sir J. M. Barrie in whose title 'The Admirable Crichton' has been 'immortalised.' Yet, despite the recent arguments of R. D. S. Jack and others that Barrie is too easily dropped from the canon of Scottish literature, it would be hard to find many among the younger generation who would consider *The Admirable Crichton* an 'immortal' play, or even to find many who have read it. The building's tenuous connection with literary canonicity is eroding. The little blue plaque serves as a reminder that the canons of different disciplines may project different values on to the same object, and that now more than ever canonicity is in flux. While it is unlikely that all copies of a literary work which ceases to be canonical will be pulped, there is a good chance that unlisted, uncanonical buildings will be demolished. The fact that canonicity can be bound up with cultural survival is one which makes debates about canons all the more passionate, and, sometimes, all the narrower.

This is particularly so in countries such as Scotland where a lack of democratic control over the nation's own affairs means that, in the absence of political institutions, cultural institutions are often regarded as the custodians of national distinctiveness. Under such circumstances it is all too easy to resort to a canon of nationalistic purity, one which automatically emphasises, for example, writing in Scots or Gaelic over literature in English. The sooner we become conscious that while canons may be useful, they are many, the sooner we will realise that the value of Scotland is bound up with the values of Scotlands.

For 'a canon' means not a literary canon, or a canon of paintings, or of *Who's Who in Scotland*; instead, it means all those things, so that there is a variety of canons within and outside Scotland, each producing a Scotland of its own. Moreover, if a canon is simply a way of uniting features or phenomena perceived as important, it can be argued that the perceptions of any group or even any individual generate a canon of deliberately or unconsciously selected features or artefacts which constitute for that group or person what matters most about Scotland.

Scotlands, then, precede, accompany, and follow Scotland. I refer not just to the vital imaginings of artists and planners, politicians and others whose dream states exist constantly beyond the actual state which would ossify without them. I mean also the way a multiplicity of groups within (and outwith) Scotland hold different views of the place, its canons, and its culture. So we have Catholic Scotland, which means not only those constituent individuals and areas of Scotland which might be identified as Catholic, but also the views of Scotland which the Catholic community holds, and which are likely, in some ways at least, to differ from those of Islamic Scotland or Protestant Scotland. So we have Gaelic Scotland, whose vision is constructed through and by the Gaelic language, we have Scots Scotland, Urdu-speaking Scotland, English-speaking Scotland. And there are Scotlands beyond our national boundaries, yet which construct their own Scotlands that in turn influence our state: the Scotlands of Japanese corporate investment, of the descendants of those cleared from the Highlands, the Scotlands of Australia and New Zealand. It is Scotlands which make Scotland for us.

Yet this idea is too simple. For not all Gaels or men or Presbyterians think alike, which means there are left-wing Gaelic feminist Scotlands and right-wing Gaelic Scotlands; there are Glaswegian technocratic revisionist Scotlands, Glaswegian communist technocratic Scotlands – there are more Scotlands than people who live in Scotland; and there are many Scotlands abroad. This is a useful if dazzling way to think, because it gets us away from the pressures for pure Scottish canons and for one essentialist Scotland that have tended to plague us because of Scotland's continuing anxiety about its political status. A nation whose culture is under pressure often clings tightly to traditional notions of itself, to emphasize purity and continuity as opposed to plurality and change, since change seems to threaten a dissolution of identity. Too many of us like to believe that there is one true Scotland, and anything else is a fake, a kailyardism, a Harry Lauderism, a sell-out to the English. The essentialist Scotland tends to be aggressively combative because it knows (though it may pretend otherwise) that it alone holds the truth, the genuine Scottishness, and it is merciless to those who betray it.

There is a growing wariness of notions of an essentialist Scotland – in the historiography of Colin Kidd, for example, and in the writings of feminist critics such as those assembled in Caroline Gonda's *Tea and Leg-Irons*.[1] It's good to see recent anthologies of poetry following MacDiarmid's lead in his *Golden Treasury of Scottish Poetry* (1940) and bringing together work in 'the languages of Scotland', aware that Scotland is and has long been an assembly of languages and cultures, a plural culture not a monoculture. It is in this climate that the work of Bakhtin has much to offer in providing models and patterns to think with which, by their unfamiliarity, may liberate us from older theoretical straitjackets and bring us into closer touch with the theoretical debates of the wider world (including those about canonicity), at the same time as offering us models which make good sense of our own culture. This is particularly appropriate in a postmodern age when in many disciplines the notion of a canon with a fixed identity seems either threatened or improbable.

To start with, Bakhtin sees identity not as fixed, closed, and unchanging, but as formed and reformed through dialogue. The self is always part of a community of selves which change, and change each other, through processes of dialogue. The self develops through contact with the other, and depends on that process of contact. It is not a monologue but a continuing series of dialogues. Such a notion of the self surely accords well with more recent formulations such as those of the Canadian philosopher Charles Taylor.

While Taylor's magisterial 1989 study *Sources of the Self: The Making of Modern Identity* makes no mention of Bakhtin or his thought, it is striking how rapidly the Bakhtinian 'dialogical self' has moved centre-stage in Taylor's 1991 book on *The Ethics of Authenticity* in which, acknowledging in particular the Bakhtin of *Problems of Dostoevsky's Poetics*, Taylor writes that

> The general feature of human life that I want to evoke is its fundamentally *dialogical* character. We become full human agents, capable of understanding ourselves, and hence of defining an identity, through our acquisition of rich human languages of expression. For purposes of this discussion, I want to take 'language' in a broad sense, covering not only the words we speak but also other modes of expression whereby we define ourselves, including the 'languages' of art, of gesture, of love, and the like. But we are inducted into these in exchange with others. No one acquires the languages needed for self-definition on their own. We are introduced to them through exchanges with others who matter to us – what George Herbert Mead called 'significant others.' The genesis of the human mind is in this sense not 'monological,' not something each accomplishes on his or her own, but dialogical.[2]

The attractiveness of this Bakhtinian approach is widely appealing, and extends far beyond those literary scholars on both sides of the Atlantic for whom Bakhtin's work is fast becoming a useful theoretical tool. It was striking that when Richard Rorty reviewed Taylor's book in early 1993 he picked out the 'dialogical self' as one of the most exciting and helpful ideas in *The Ethics of Authenticity*. Rorty points out that as regards being 'true to ourselves'

> Taylor says . . . we should keep reminding people that the selves to which they hope to be true are 'dialogical selves' – that we are what we are because of the people, real or imaginary, with whom we have talked. . . . None of us has a self to be faithful to except the one which has been cobbled together in interchanges with parents and siblings, friends and enemies, churches and governments. Even if we bring something new into the world, it will be at best a slight modification of what was already there. Being authentic to ourselves, is being faithful to something which was produced in collaboration with a lot of other people.[3]

Though Bakhtin's name has vanished in Rorty's account, it is striking how much this contemporary and readily comprehensible view of the self has emerged from Bakhtin's work, as the phrase 'dialogical selves' indicates, and as the stressed primacy on social language emphasizes. Whatever its sometimes rebarbative properties, important aspects of Bakhtin's thought are rapidly acquiring a wide currency. In a Scottish context, and in the context of canonicity, this may have particular benefits.

For canons and cultures as well as persons are the products of dialogue, and the Bakhtinian emphasis on dialogue applies also to societies, not just to individuals. Certainly it applies to the way in which one society and its body of knowledge relates to and is shaped by another. So, for instance in the 'Response to a Question from the *Novy Mir* Editorial Staff' Bakhtin points out that

There exists a very strong, but one-sided and thus untrustworthy, idea that in order better to understand a foreign culture, one must enter into it, forgetting one's own, and view the world through the eyes of this foreign culture. This idea, as I said, is one-sided. Of course, a certain entry as a living being into a foreign culture, the possibility of seeing the world through its eyes, is a necessary part of the process of understanding it; but if this were the only aspect of this understanding, it would merely be duplication and would not entail anything new or enriching. *Creative understanding* does not renounce itself, its own place in time, its own culture; and it forgets nothing. In order to understand, it is immensely important for the person who understands to be *located outside* the object of his or her creative understanding – in time, in space, in culture. For one cannot even really see one's own exterior and comprehend it as a whole, and no mirrors or photographs can help; our real exterior can be seen and understood only by other people, because they are located outside us in space and because they are *others*.

In the realm of culture, outsideness is a most powerful factor in understanding. It is only in the eyes of *another* culture that foreign culture reveals itself fully and profoundly (but not maximally fully, because there will be cultures that see and understand even more). A meaning only reveals its depths once it has encountered and come into contact with another, foreign meaning: they engage in a kind of dialogue, which surmounts the closedness and one-sidedness of these particular meanings, these cultures. We raise new questions for a foreign culture, ones that it did not raise itself; we seek answers to our own questions in it; and the foreign culture responds to us by revealing to us its new aspects and new semantic depths. Without *one's own* questions one cannot creatively understand anything other or foreign (but, of course, the questions must be serious and sincere). Such a dialogic encounter of two cultures does not result in merging or mixing. Each retains its own unity and *open* totality, but they are mutually enriched.[4]

I make no apology for quoting this substantial passage which I have already quoted in my book *Identifying Poets* where I was writing at length of the importance of Bakhtin for Scottish and other literary studies.[5] I make no apology, because this is a passage with much to offer to many branches of cultural studies, not just to literary understanding.

It can speak to us, for instance, of the way in which canons in various fields and cultures may be produced and modified through dialogue, not least through dialogue with one another. It may be, for instance, that the literary critic who begins to look at texts regarded as canonical in Women's Studies, or features of works held to be in an important tradition of painting, may return to his or her own 'field' with certain perceptions which modify both the accepted boundaries of that field and its canon. Similarly, read in a Scottish context, Bakhtin makes clear the importance of fully internationalizing Scottish studies. The passage just quoted can speak to us not only of the way in which Scotland might be confidently open to the world beyond, but also of how within Scotland those various Scotlands may enter into dialogue, constituting the assembly of Scotland without annihilating their individual differences. And it does make sense to talk here of Scotland, rather than of the wider amalgam of Great Britain, for the mutual awareness of cultural differences (primarily between various native languages) is quite different in Scotland or in Wales from the overall awareness in Britain, where matters such as Gaelic or Welsh are totally ignored or marginalized as quaint side-shows. The linguistic and cultural pluralism of and in Scotland is significantly removed from that of England or of Britain as a whole.

It seems also that Bakhtin's thought accords well with other aspects of Scottish culture. Certainly his sense of 'other tongues', of language as composed of languages, of one speaker using and reaccenting elements from another's speech, and of the fructifying impurity of speech accords well with the heteroglossic condition of Scotland with its rich mutual interference of dialects and tongues. What Scot with an interest in language has never sensed that 'one's own language is never single language'? Bakhtin's sense of both heteroglossia and polyglossia sends us back to such figures as the Admirable Crichton, John Leyden, Scott, and Sir Thomas Urquhart (translator of Bakhtin's beloved Rabelais) with a refreshing perspective, at the same time as pointing us towards such contemporaries as Liz Lochhead, Alasdair Gray, Tom Leonard and the Edwin Morgan who has found Bakhtinian ideas congenial.[6] Some of Bakhtin's potential for Scottish literary studies was evident at the April 1993 symposium on Bakhtin and Scottish Literature held at St Andrews, where it was notable that, rather than slavishly following Bakhtin's prose-centred criticism, several contributors (J. C. Bittenbender on Burns, Roderick Watson on Goodsir Smith, Christopher Whyte on Fergusson and Burns) applied Bakhtin's ideas productively to Scottish poetry.[7] I think we may begin to add to studies of Bakhtin and individual Scottish writers a wider attempt to look from a Bakhtinian perspective at other patterns in Scottish culture.[8] Certainly the Bakhtin who in *Rabelais and his World* examined how the ribaldries of medieval and renaissance carnival co-existed with the authority of the Church may help explain to us the apparent oddity of the libertine Burns who becomes the canonically central bard of a fundamentally Presbyterian nation and whose praises have been sung often by Church of Scotland ministers.[9] Yet there are also wider cultural forms, such as the General Assembly itself – that many-tongued dialogic body – which Bakhtin may prompt us to re-view. I would suggest that, consciously or not, we tend to have a canon of distinctive Scottish cultural icons, including, for example, the Scottish legal and educational systems, the Scottish Enlightenment and the Scottish Renaissance. Bakhtin's ideas encourage us to review all of these in productive ways.

For instance, Bakhtin may encourage us to find new life in the thinking of the Scottish Enlightenment, for if Bakhtin is preoccupied by the self as social, seen and constructed by others, then this focus is shared with the Adam Smith of *The Theory of Moral Sentiments*, fascinated by attempts to see ourselves as others see us and to maintain a social, mutual identity which counters or complements the increasing atomization involved in the division of labour. Where Smith writes of self and others as linked through 'sympathy', Bakhtin emphasises the importance of 'sympathetic understanding'.[10] Common sense as mutual awareness is crucial to Bakhtin whose ideas sit well in the alien arena of Scottish Enlightenment thinking about civic virtue, mutuality and the close bonds between self and other. Bakhtin is at once alien and familiar. That combination may allow us to think with him in ways that re-energize some of our canonical cultural forms.

Not least, this is apparent in the area of education. It is dangerously close to a truism that in school and in university Scottish education continues to emphasize, at secondary and undergraduate levels, breadth rather than mere specialization. Such an emphasis means little unless all involved in the process of learning are alert to the ways in which they are part of a dialogic process. I am thinking here not simply of dialogue between students, between teachers, between students and teachers, though all these are vital; I am thinking also of that generalist tradition which George Davie celebrated in *The Democratic Intellect* and *The Crisis of the Democratic Intellect*. If one of the strengths of the Scottish educational system is that students may study a number of subjects each of which may illuminate the others in often strange ways, then all involved in the system must be aware of its dialogic nature – must be aware of ways in which, like individuals and like cultures, different disciplines and their disputed canons may illuminate, interrogate and complicate one another. Without such a dialogic sense, our education system becomes virtually meaningless as a *system*, though it may still teach isolated subjects and skills. But with such a dialogic awareness about the system come not just transferable skills (e.g. the utilization in a French class of logical and expository skills learned by the student in a class on computer programming), but also mutually-illuminating perspectives – the way in which the development of abstract computer languages may provide analogies with an insight into the development of structuralism in anthropology, for instance. A student or teacher alert to and making use of the implicitly dialogic nature of the Scottish education system is likely to be more original and flexible than one who remains unconscious of the system's possibilities. For it is a system which encourages interdisciplinary dialogue of a potentially fundamental nature. It is no accident that in earlier days philosophy functioned as a bridging mechanism between canons and disciplines, giving rise to an emphasis on theories of knowledge and on what J. F. Ferrier christened 'epistemology'. If George Davie originally intended to conclude *The Democratic Intellect* with a chapter on the St Andrews classicist John Burnet, it was because of Burnet's emphasis on the importance of what Bakhtin calls the 'dialogic' nature of knowledge, and because Burnet was aware of the way in which canons alter and intersect with each other.

Read by T. S. Eliot, D. H. Lawrence and other literary figures, Burnet (1863–1928) was a classicist of international reputation with a strong commitment to Scottish culture (he turned down the chair of Greek at Harvard in order to remain at St Andrews).[11] Championed by Davie for his commitment to the Scottish generalist tradition, Burnet had explored the history of Scottish university education. He was particularly eager to maintain an awareness of the links between classical culture, poetry, and science, and emphasized that 'we must try to remember that every department of knowledge has its universal side, the side on which it comes into touch with every other, and that is the most important side of it for the educator'.[12] This stress on dialogue between subjects and on interdisciplinary boundaries allows us to relate Burnet's Scottish humanist ideals not only to the tradition in Scottish university education which stresses the centrality of philosophy and the principles of knowledge, but also to the Bakhtinian emphasis on dialogue between subjects with a view to mutual illumination. Though Davie makes no mention of Bakhtin, it is valuable to juxtapose with the long quotation from Bakhtin above Davie's admiration for the way in which

> . . . in Burnet's account of the origins of Greek philosophy . . . the moment of illumination comes when the traveller notes a foreign group to be very different in one particular department of its life . . . as compared with his own group, though in other departments of life . . . it might be very similar. Before making this discovery, the traveller did not, indeed could not, make this distinction in regard to his own group.[13]

In other words, knowledge and self-knowledge grows out of contact with the other. Davie may exaggerate the exciting qualities of Burnet's writing. For all his awareness of Ferrier and of interdisciplinary links, Burnet in his *Essays and Addresses* particularly seems too often anecdotal and dated. Yet, even if Davie's own paean to generalism can be over-rhapsodic and can partake of intellectual myth-making, the blending of myth and scholarship functions to alert us to a strength in Scottish intellectual life and one which accords well with the non-Scottish perspective of Bakhtin. When Davie praises *A Drunk Man Looks at the Thistle* for reminding us through 'reviving the forgotten doctrine of Adam Smith, Schelling and Hegel that self-consciousness is inseparable from mutual consciousness', he points us again towards the importance of what Bakhtin calls 'the dialogic'.[14] Philosophy and 'General Theory' have long since ceased to be core elements of our Scottish degree structure. But a conscious awareness and discussion of the dialogic nature of self and of learning might help restore a sense of the enormous potential in the system, and might serve as a simple epistemological bridge giving greater cohesion and distinctiveness to the degree structure. Unless the traditional Scottish educational system rediscovers and clearly articulates the dialogic strengths of its structure, it does not deserve to survive. At the time of writing the curricular pattern and degree structure within Scottish universities remains among the core canon of characteristic Scottish institutions. It seems at least possible that an increasing awareness of Bakhtinian arguments will strengthen and modify such a position.

This would be particularly timely in a period when several universities are developing interdisciplinary Scottish Studies institutes in which dialogue between subjects, individuals and established or disestablished canons may flourish. It is essential that, while such institutes concentrate on Scotland and Scotlands, they remain open to the wider world of debate, not least to the wider worlds of cultural theory. It is dangerously easy for those involved in the culture of a small country to fail to raise their eyes to the horizon, and to wish to look only towards home-grown interpretative models. Neither Adam Smith nor Hugh MacDiarmid manifested an interest in such chauvinistic self-sufficiency. Nor should we. I hope that, like that cultural icon, the Admirable Crichton, *Scotlands* may further an awareness of the pluralist inheritances and potential of Scotland, as well as the ways in which those may be interpreted. Most of all I hope that the magazine may encourage dialogues in a Bakhtinian spirit.

Such dialogues are likely to run across and interfere with established academic boundaries in fruitful ways which may complement and turn to advantage the uncertain status of various disciplinary canons. What I am arguing for in this article is simple, yet basic. Though Scotland itself, and several key areas of its culture (among them literature and the educational system) are clearly dialogic in nature we too often fail to be alert to the strengths of this position. As a writer Bakhtin can be offputting, participating (in some texts more than others) in those dialects of professional obfuscation which Pierre Bourdieu sees as bound up with 'homo academicus'.[15] Yet a real engagement with Bakhtin's thought is likely to send us back to some of our key cultural institutions with a new sense both of their nature and their potential. Dialogues between, for example, Dunbar or Burns or Scott and Bakhtin, or between Scottish religion or Scottish education and Bakhtin are likely to yield further Scotlands which will quicken our native culture and open it again to the wider world of cultures and of theories beyond. *Scotlands* and the growing international interest in interdisciplinary Scottish studies may function as part of that process. I hope that readers of this first issue may begin to see already links between the various canons and canonical questions discussed, using the Bakhtinian notion of dialogue and the self as composed through dialogue as a way of moving among and inter-connecting the various Scotlands here set forth. More than that, I hope that an increasing familiarity with the work of Bakhtin may help generate new views and interpretative models of Scottish culture and the interplay between its various canons and forms, working with rather than against their dialogic nature. 🏵

University of St Andrews

1 An example of Colin Kidd's work appears elsewhere in this issue of *Scotlands*; Caroline Gonda, ed., *Tea and Leg-Irons*(London: Open Letters, 1992).

2 Charles Taylor, *The Ethics of Authenticity* (Cambridge, Mass: Harvard University Press, 1991), p. 32.

3 Richard Rorty, 'In a Flattened World,' *London Review of Books*, 8 April 1993, p. 3; Rorty is reviewing Taylor's *The Ethics of Authority*.

4 M. M. Bakhtin, 'Response to a Question from the *Novy Mir* Editorial Staff' in *Speech Genres and Other Late Essays*, translated by Vern W. McGee, edited by Caryl Emerson and Michael Holquist (Austin: University of Texas Press, 1986), pp. 6–7.

5 Robert Crawford, *Identifying Poets: Self and Territory in Twentieth-Century Poetry* (Edinburgh: Edinburgh University Press, 1993); see especially the Introduction which suggests some directions from which Bakhtin's work may be approached in a Scottish context.

6 See Crawford, *Identifying Poets*, pp. 10 and 177–78 (n.33).

7 This symposium was organized by J. C. Bittenbender (who is writing a doctoral thesis at St Andrews on Bakhtin and Scottish literature) and by the present writer. Several of these papers are about to be published. A notable aspect of the symposium was the discussion led by Dr Pam Morris (Department of English, University of Dundee) on using Bakhtin in teaching Scottish literature. Dr Morris's forthcoming Bakhtin reader is likely to make Bakhtin's work more readily available for classroom use.

8 Some earlier articles which relate Bakhtin to individual Scottish writers include:

Deanna Delmar Evans, 'Dunbar's *Tretis*: The Seven Deadly Sins in Carnivalesque Disguise', *Neophilologus* 73 (1989), pp. 130–41.

Ruth Grogan, 'W. S. Graham: A Dialogical Imagination', *English Studies* in Canada, Vol. 15 No. 2 (June 1989), pp. 196–213.

Carol McGuirk, 'Burns, Bakhtin, and the Opposition of Poetic and Novelistic Discourse: A Response to David Morris' [see below], *The Eighteenth Century: Theory and Interpretation*, Vol. 32 No. 1 (Spring 1991), pp. 58–72.

David B. Morris, 'Burns and Heteroglossia', *The Eighteenth Century: Theory and Interpretation*, Vol. 28 No. 1 (Winter, 1987), pp. 3–27.

I am grateful to J. C. Bittenbender and Christopher MacLachlan for drawing these articles to my attention. On Scott and Bakhtin see Ina Ferris, *The Achievement of Literary Authority: Gender, History, and the Waverley Novels* (Ithaca: Cornell University Press, 1991), pp. 130–33 and 191–92. There is much work to be done in this area.

9 Mikhail Bakhtin, *Rabelais and His World*, translated by Hélène Iswolsky (1968; rpt. Bloomington: Indiana University Press, 1984).

10 M. M. Bakhtin, *Art and Answerability: Early Philosophical Essays*, ed. Michael Holquist and Vadim Liapunov, translated by Vadim Liapunov (Austin: University of Texas Press, 1990), p. 102.

11 John Burnet, *Essays and Addresses* (London: Chatto and Windus, 1929), p. 16 ('Memoir' by Lord Charnwood).

12 Burnet, *Essays and Addresses*, p. 125 ('Humanism in Education').

13 George Davie, *The Crisis of the Democratic Intellect* (Edinburgh: Polygon, 1986), p. 73.

14 *Ibid.*, p. 136.

15 Pierre Bourdieu, *Homo Academicus*, translated by Peter Collier (Cambridge: Polity Press, 1988).

DAVID HILL RADCLIFFE

Education, imitation and the romantic canon

Proponents and opponents of change alike discuss English literature as though it were the collective memory of a nation, sex or minority group. The memory metaphor implies a 'unity of mind' in literatures assembled by many minds over long periods of time. What is usually at issue is less memory than education: teachers must confront collections of texts (and students) that are selective, mutable and diverse. The notion of collective memory explains little about either the impressive continuity of English literature or its equally impressive capacity for change, both products of educational practices that differ from time to time and place to place. The kinds of continuity scholars and teachers discover in the past tends to reflect their perceptions of discontinuity in the present.

Robert Crawford calls attention to how 'Scots in particular were crucially instrumental in constructing the university subject of English literature itself.[1] 'English' literature was invented in Scotland because eighteenth-century Scots had pressing reasons for defining what it means to be 'British'. The example raises two questions: if 'English Literature' post-dates literature in English by several centuries, should works written before and after this event be taught in the same way? If English literature and British literature are not identical, should their differences make a difference in the way literature is taught? I would answer 'yes' to both questions, because teaching literature in English as English Literature – as collective memory to be internalized through aesthetic empathy – obscures the kinds of social, historical and geographical collectivity that English literature was and is. Attending to historical and geographical differences helps students learn to locate themselves as agents in complex and changing collective structures.

English Literature was invented to recast social differences in psychological terms, giving rise to aesthetic education. The social differences aesthetic education was invented to reconcile were not only national, but sexual, political, religious and economic – the full range of phenomena we now describe as 'cultural'. It is no accident that the concept of culture enters the critical vocabulary contemporaneously with the invention of English Literature, or that both appear to originate in Scotland.[2] With all of us engaged in the process of rethinking issues of social difference, we could do worse than re-examine the differences that literary education made (and concealed) two hundred years ago. How did aesthetic doctrine recast the older practice of imitation and what has this implied for subsequent practices and critical dilemmas?

I will discuss these matters in conjunction with imitations of Shakespeare and Spenser by writers – Scottish, Irish, and English – engaged in inventing what we now call 'culture'. That Shakespeare and Spenser meant different things to different people goes without saying; what needs saying is that imitation was crucial to the formation of English studies at a time when literary imitation is not supposed to matter.[3] By reopening the question of imitation in romantic poetry we can better understand not only why educators differed over Spenser and Shakespeare but how the neglect of latter-day imitations has obfuscated the historicity of English studies and obscured the place of many of the writers instrumental in inventing it. Imitation has been treated as a failure of originality and as a threat to liberal values, yet 'originality' emerged from a search for national origins and modern 'liberalism' owes much to imitations of Spenser and Shakespeare.

When Americans think of the canon, we think of the *Norton Anthology of English Literature* (first edition, 1962), not only because so many of us teach it and were taught by it, but because it is marked by a strong, Biblical understanding of 'canon'. *Norton* disposes its contents into a sequence of periods, each operating under its own dispensation, but all tending towards a final illumination. Prefaces and headnotes draw parallels to social history, assisting the reader to follow the march of literature and society towards liberal democracy. *Norton* is divided into two testaments, one governed by the law of imitation, the other by the grace of originality, though the former contains many types and foreshadowings of the latter. Standing at the centre of the vast edifice is the Romantic Revolution, first announced by its prophet William Blake. William Wordsworth delivers the new gospel in the preface to *Lyrical Ballads* which, like the Sermon on the Mount, liberates readers and writers from the tyranny of the Law, offering to all a new dispensation of love and reconciliation.

Like the Bible, the structure of this secular canon is partly historical accretion, partly reconstruction after the fact. For similar reasons, its prophetic structure has been subject to intense critical, historical and editorial scrutiny—and with similar results. Blake and Wordsworth, of course, can be shown to be products of the eighteenth century as surely as Jesus was a rabbi, though the significance of this is disputed. Historical criticism has revealed the presence of romantic sects – Lake Poets, Cockney Poets, Satanic Poets – whose relation to the central revelation is explored and debated. And most recently, feminist scholarship has discovered – lo! – that women played a crucial role in formulating and disseminating the romantic gospel, a role later suppressed by institutionalizing patriarchs.[4] The canon is under revision, with changes announced for the new *Norton*.

This or future editions are not likely to challenge the centrality of romanticism, which would require a thorough reconceptualization of English Studies. It would require more than changing the canon, for the idea of a 'canon' in the *Norton* sense is itself a romantic construct. It would need to be something other than ideology critique, for 'ideology' is a romantic construct. It would entail something other than a search for mothers and madwomen, for the treatment of influence as family romance is a romantic construct. It would need to be something other than cultural studies, for 'culture' is the keystone in romantic understandings of selfhood, education, politics and sociology. Such radical change would be unthinkable, were there not precedents for it in the revival of the classics during the Renaissance, and the invention of English Studies during the era we call romantic.

Romantic critics, for whom 'romantic' meant in the manner of Ariosto or Spenser, frequently drew comparisons between their own time and the Renaissance, as in a *Blackwoods* essay (August, 1824) that speaks of 'the distinguished fraternity of bards, of whom our country is so justly proud, and who have united in forming of the reigns of George the Third and Fourth another Age of Genius, only second to that of Elizabeth' (162). Like *Norton*, this critic regards contemporary writers as an improvement over the last generation, 'imitators of imitators – the third pressing of an exhausted wine-press – the ninth and dwindled farrow of the school of Pope and Addison' (163). Where he differs from *Norton* is in his sense of who these original geniuses were, for he lived in a time when Blake was not known, Shelley a marginal figure, Kirke White was preferred to Keats, and Wordsworth was more respected than read. The view from Edinburgh in 1824 is consequently rather different from that in Ithaca in 1962; launching a new series on 'Celebrated Female Writers,' *Blackwoods* canonizes Joanna Baillie as the spirit of the age.

Making allowances for overstatement, the claim that 'every one of the master spirits, who have arisen into subsequent celebrity, have received, almost as boys, the impressions of her genius, and have either avowedly or unconsciously followed in the track marked out by her example' is not entirely improbable, for almost all of them are on record as admirers of her work.[5] Only with the belated establishment of Wordsworth as the Great Romantic would Baillie's star set, and even then under the sway of critical beliefs that she herself did much to establish. The *Blackwoods* retrospective sets out several themes I will pursue in discussing imitation in romantic poetry: the Elizabethan precedent, the centrality of women writers ('humiliating to the pretensions of the stronger sex'), the significance of James Beattie's *Minstrel* ('incomparably the best work from the hand of any living writer' when Baillie began writing), and the significance of forming a 'national poetry' (162). Not one of these themes figures in the *Norton* account of British romanticism (2:1–20).[6]

The neglect of these topics probably stems from a programmatic attempt to correlate 'originality' with the French Revolution. The romantics themselves more often located their origins in a renaissance of the Renaissance: 'In our Augustan age, we see the mind of the country tending with determined force *from* that ancient [British] literature; and these later days we have seen it returning upon the treasures of those older times, with an almost passionate admiration' (*Blackwoods*, Dec. 1818, 264). The Augustans neglected the well of English undefiled to follow in the classicizing footsteps of hated France. In response, British critics developed an alternative canon and alternative ways of reading and teaching it. The triumph of 'romanticism' may be dated from Richard Hurd's *Letters on Chivalry and Romance* (1761), Joseph Warton's *Essay on the Writings and Genius of Pope* (1756, 1782), Thomas Warton's *Observations on the Fairy Queen* (1754, 1762) and *History of English Poetry* (1774–81), and Clara Reeve's *Progress of Romance* (1785), works whose appearance coincides with scholarly editions of Spenser (Upton, 1758; Todd, 1805), Raleigh (1751), Drayton (1748, 1753), William Browne (1772), Giles and Phineas Fletcher (1783), and anthologies of early poetry by Bell (1778), Anderson (1792), Ellis (1801), and Chalmers (1810). Romantic readers, who identified poetry with passion and romance with admiration, felt 'passionate admiration' for a literature opposed to both the common sense of the British Enlightenment and the scepticism of the French.[7]

It was, however, no simple matter to present Renaissance poetry in opposition to imitation, because so much of it was devoted to imitating classical antiquity. In order to revive Spenser, Shakespeare and Milton, English studies needed to undermine the pedagogical programme that produced Spenser, Shakespeare and Milton. The early romantics were all humanist-trained and many, like Gray, Smart and the Wartons, were academics thems[ ][8] Critics and educators adopted two strategies for disentangling Renai[ ] poetry from imitation, both involving 'genius.' Small Latin and less G[ ] came selling points for untutored Shakespeare. Lesser Elizabethans[ ] con-demned for their ignorance of the rules, were now admired for '[ ]rity' or 'simplicity.' Growing out of this revaluation of decorum and p[ ]ity, a second concept of genius referred not to individuals but the age: R[ ]ce poetry was recast as 'Gothic,' an expression of the genius of Britis[ ].

Early romantics looked to the Age of Elizabeth as the model for a liberal, virtuous and militantly Protestant nation.

Perhaps the single most important attempt to come to grips with these issues is James Beattie's *The Minstrel; or The Progress of Genius* (1771, 1774). The poem is significant for a number of reasons. Beattie worked his way up through the Scottish educational system as a scholarship student, usher, schoolmaster and college professor. The *Minstrel* consists of 'some thoughts on education' by one of the very few college professors of the era who made a mark as a teacher. The poem continues Beattie's self-declared war on the Frenchified David Hume. For all its limitations as poetry, the *Minstrel* taught generations of romantic poets how to educate their genius, Wordsworth particularly. The *Minstrel* taught romantic writers how to imitate without imitating, though Beattie himself stopped writing poetry rather than pursue the path he had marked out for others to follow.

The two cantos of the poem develop opposing views of education. In the first, Edwin cultivates imagination and piety through untutored encounters with rainbows, fairies, ballads and old wive's tales. On this account, British minstrelsy can be seen as an entirely native production, a natural eruption of native genius unsullied by contact with classical authorities. In the second canto, however, innocent Edwin encounters a morose hermit singing the woes of experience. The hermit-schoolmaster insists that Edwin discipline his woodnotes wild by submitting to a proper training in the arts and sciences. The ensuing dialogue opposes innocence to experience, with Edwin making the Rousseauvian case: 'Ah, what have I to do with conquering kings . . . To those, whom Nature has taught to think and feel, / Heroes, alas! are things of small concern' (2:35).[9] The hermit extols discipline: to 'frame those forms of bright perfection' (2:58), minstrels require knowledge of history, theology, moral philosophy and natural science – science as articulated in *The Faerie Queene* and *Paradise Lost*, as taught by Beattie himself in Aberdeen.

Beattie knew well enough that 'the progress of genius' in British poetry had been driven by humanism; at the same time, with Rousseau, he yearns for the 'primeval grove' where 'To all an equal lot Heaven's bounty gave' (2:38), innocent times before progress and economic specialization introduced inequality and vice. The *Minstrel* gropes towards an innovative practice of imitation that might enable progress without the harmful effects of social differentiation. This finds expression in Beattie's poetics, a sea-change in British Spenserianism: 'I have endeavoured to imitate Spenser in the measure of his verse, and in the harmony, simplicity, and variety of his composition. Antique expressions I have avoided; admitting, however, some old words, where they seemed to suit the subject' (p. 3). Substituting an unspecific poetic diction for Spenser's archaicisms, the poet avoids the decorums of place, time and social rank observed by humanist imitators. In place of discrimination, we have 'spirit,' as in Beattie's defense of the Spenserian stanza: 'It pleases my ear, and seems, from its Gothic structure and original, to bear some relation to the subject and spirit of the Poem. It admits both simplicity and magnificence of sound and language' (p. 4). Beattie turns to the gothic as a means of imagining a just and unified society, one that combines simplicity and magnificence, untutored genius and elevated conception.

Beattie's usage follows Montesquieu's *Spirit of the Laws* (1748), which had found in Gothic 'spirit' a principle of social organization that binds complex societies together.[10] On the hermit's account, it is a minstrel's responsibility to promote this harmony through song: "Tis he alone, whose comprehensive mind, / From situation, temper, soil, and clime / Explored, a nation's various powers can bind, / And various orders, in one form sublime / Of polity' (2:55). The 'Gothic structure and original' of Spenser's stanza is equivalent to the spirit of the Ancient Constitution, usurped by the French Plantagenets ('Spoil, carnage, and the cruel pomp of pride; / chant of heraldry the drowsy song,' 2:36). In the *Minstrel*, as in Gray's 'The Bard', imitating the Elizabethans is tantamount to reconstituting the 'spirit' of the British constitution ('The voice of the Eternal said, Be free,' 2:31).[11] But if genius or spirit is what is peculiar to the 'situation, temper, soil, and clime' of a nation, Renaissance poetry can no longer be regarded as a stage in the progress towards Dryden and Pope. Rather, the progress of genius is the resurrection of liberty, a renaissance without imitation, even as Beattie imitates the spirit rather than the letter of Spenser's poem.

We have, then, a political rationale for a new canon of English literature, a poetics that projects unifying spirit rather than divisive decorum, and the beginnings of a pedagogy that subordinates imitation to genius. The latter proved the stumbling block, because it was far from clear how an untutored villager like Edwin could command the comprehensive vision a just society requires from its poetic legislators, or, on the other hand, how an educated bard in a complex modern society could unite innocence and experience, low and high, the primitive with the progressive. More clearly than any other poem of its time the *Minstrel* articulates the categories and the contradictions on which 'English literature' was founded.

The *Minstrel* was probably the most highly regarded long poem written in the second half of the eighteenth century. Its influence on Wordsworth and Byron is well known, but mostly forgotten are the scores of Spenser imitations from untutored geniuses written in its wake, poems written by lower-class authors who educated themselves by reading poetry in English: Burns, Thelwall, Turnbull, Dermody, Struthers, White, Barton and Clare. These poets describe village piety and superstition like so many Edwins come to life. Beattie's account of extracurricular education encouraged the semi-literate to write and encouraged the literate to attend to their writings as manifestations of a liberal British spirit. Beattie's effect on the other class of untutored geniuses – women poets – is more difficult to gauge. While their stocks in trade are *Minstrel*-like piety, sentiment and patriotism, the Spenserian stanza is less common in their poetry.

It is, however, the stanza of the Irish Mary Tighe's *Psyche* (1805, written perhaps a decade earlier). Anglo-Irish writers took eighteenth-century Spenserianism to its extremes, though the usual Protestant tub-thumping is absent from *Psyche*.[12] Tighe's poem is remembered today for Keats's sneer: 'Mrs Tighe and Beattie once delighted me – now I see through them and can find nothing in them – or weakness – and yet how many they still delight!'[13] What Keats 'saw through' is likely their didacticism and commitment to imitation. Ross discusses why writers like Tighe valued community in ways that precluded Keatsian originality and how this subsequently damaged their reputations (158–67). Yet Tighe's progress of love *is* original within modern Spenserianism: it is a poem about education that does not imitate the Rousseauvian *Minstrel* and a poem about manners that does not imitate the Augustan *Castle of Indolence*. Tighe's originality lies in a return to Spenser as a moral teacher. *Psyche* is a more knowing imitation of Spenserian moral allegory than can be found in any eighteenth-century poem, much less any romantic poem. Tighe, plainly the mistress of a classical education, offers a thoroughly Aristotelian treatment of feminine virtues and vices: Meekness, Constancy, Chastity, Patience; Pride, Inconstancy, Loose-Delight, Spleen. Despite its glowing diction and erotic subject matter, despite even its 'Knight of the Bleeding Heart', *Psyche* is a poem about making discriminations and disciplining the affections.

The significance of this didactic programme can be seen if we compare *Psyche* to the *Minstrel*: Tighe has followed the hermit's lead and moralized her song. She is the untutored writer trained in humanist discipline. Arguably, she could complete her 'progress' where Beattie failed *because* she was a woman writing to women. *Psyche* is entirely concerned with domestic affairs, and therefore avoids the issues in political economy that were rendering humanism unworkable in public life. Because she is not attempting to cement a social polity at war with France, she can treat 'virtue' in ways that are class and gender specific: 'Nor scorn the lighter labours of the muse, / Who yet, for cruel battles would not dare / The low-strung chords of her weak lyre prepare' (1812, p. 5). Yet this apology, and others, frame her return to Renaissance pedagogy as mere fancy, as faerie-londe. The six cantos begin and end with stanzas that use aesthetic discourse to situate the poem in relation to author and readers, acknowledging (as had Spenser) the separation of ideal and real, Albion from Britain. No doubt it was this imaginative play, and not the morality it frames, that appealed so to young Keats and his contemporaries.

Psyche and the *Minstrel* illustrate how humanist ideals of education survive under stress in romantic poetry; in what follows I examine two critical prefaces that situate Renaissance humanism in different and opposing terms. Wordsworth's preface to *Lyrical Ballads* (1800, 1802) engages the same pedagogical issues as the poems by Beattie and Tighe. *Norton* describes the Preface as an 'attempt to overturn the reigning tradition . . . deserv[ing] its reputation as a turning point in English literature' (2:6). Its 'canonical' status could hardly be higher: 'Wordsworth and his visionary fellow poets set out to revise the Biblical promise of divine redemption by reconstituting the grounds of hope and pronouncing the coming of a time in which a renewed humanity will inhabit a renovated earth on which men and women will feel thoroughly at home' (2:7). It was out of 'democratic sympathies', we are told, that Wordsworth 'undertook to overthrow the basic theory, as well as the reigning practice, of neoclassic poetry' (159). But Wordsworth nowhere praises democracy, nor, in criticizing Gray's Spenserian diction, is he attacking neoclassicism.[14] Rather, like Beattie or Tighe, he attempts to modify humanist imitation to make it work within changed circumstances.

Wordsworth is opposed to revolutions. While he recognizes that 'metrical language must in different areas of literature have excited very different expectations', change is not good, particularly in commercial societies where poetry is bought and sold like a commodity: 'It will appear to many persons that I have not fulfilled the terms of an engagement thus voluntarily contracted' (155).[15] Wordsworth can violate this contract with impunity not because fashions change but because poetry has a second, non-contractual basis in the passions. By *resisting* 'revolutions not of literature alone, but likewise of society itself', he can produce a class of poetry 'well adapted to interest mankind permanently' (154–55). Wordsworth associates revolution with the round of luxury, levelling and corruption; it threatens 'to blunt the discriminating powers of the mind, and unfitting it for all voluntary exertion to reduce it to a state of almost savage torpor' (160). The Preface does not attack the neoclassic hierarchy of genres; it does attack a failure to discriminate between 'frantic novels' and 'elder writers, I had almost said the works of Shakespear and Milton' (160). Wordsworth takes note of the changes celebrated in *Norton*, and rejects them emphatically.

Those engaged in commerce neglect literature of permanent interest because they live in cities 'where the uniformity of their occupations produces a craving for extraordinary incident' (160). The problem is not that all occupations are similar, but that divisions of labour reduce occupations to the rote repetition of a few simple actions. So, far from being uniform, society is devolving into a fragmented and rapidly changing complex without a sense of the whole and consequently without political virtue. This is the state of affairs that provoked Beattie's visionary evocation of poor but innocent

Scotland; like Beattie, Wordsworth looks to the rural past in an attempt to redefine how education might function in the urban present. He must also confront Beattie's progeny, imitating untutored genius without falling into the 'triviality and meanness' (157) of the would-be Edwins hymning village virtue in vulgar verse. An 1815 letter takes aim at the Ettrick Shepherd's unlettered Spenserians: 'if there is to be an Error in style, I much prefer the *Classical* model of Dr. Beattie to the insupportable slovenliness and neglect of syntax and grammar, by which Hogg's writings are disfigured.'[16]

Wordsworth's rather sophisticated response to the dilemma posed by Beattie has been badly misrepresented by those who have taken the 'man speaking to men' to imply everyman speaking to anyone. Like Mary Tighe, Wordsworth looks back to an Aristotelian and humanist pedagogy. To become a good poet (as to become a good lover) it is necessary to cultivate a proper disposition. As Wordsworth is at pains to emphasize, this is not the affair of a moment but the 'purpose' of a lifetime. In the *Norton* account, 'the free activity of the imagination' arises 'from impulse, and free from all rules and the artful manipulation of means to foreseen ends' (2:8). By 'spontaneous', of course, Wordsworth means not free but unconscious: 'obeying blindly and mechanically the impulses of those habits' (158). This understanding of 'moral relations' (154) as habits and dispositions derives from accounts of the virtues in elder writers like Aristotle in the *Nichomachean Ethics* or Spenser in *The Faerie Queene*. By means of an artful regimen of contemplative discipline the poet can 'describe objects and utter sentiments of such a nature and in such connection with each other, that the understanding of the being to whom we address ourselves, if he be in a healthful state of association, must necessarily be in some degree enlightened, his taste exalted, and his affections ameliorated' (158). Note the survival of the humanist triplicate: instruct, amuse, move.

Beattie got into trouble when he attempted to identify untutored apprehension with the humanist's emphasis on training and discipline. Wordsworth circumvents this difficulty by rearranging the site of instruction: the hermit goes to school with the villager and he, not 'Edwin', becomes the poet. The result is reconstituted pastoral, low like its matter but high like the learned traditions in which the poet writes. Nor should there be any mistake about the humanist traditions this 'new Poete' invokes: like Spenser in the *Shepheards Calendar*, he launches a career by recasting the language of poetry and using pastoral to criticize corruption. This is no project for an untutored villager. Passages excised from *Norton* stress the artfulness of ballad imitations 'entirely separate . . . from the vulgarity and meanness of ordinary life' (164), underscoring (with a nod towards Reynolds's *Discourses*) that taste 'is an *acquired* talent, which can only be produced by thought and a long intercourse with the best models of composition' (177).

Why then does Wordsworth imitate incidents of 'common' life rather than the conventional moral subjects? Because he is recasting civic humanism: rather than write poems about politics, he regards poetry *as* politics: 'among the qualities which I have enumerated as principally conducing to form a Poet, is implied nothing differing in kind from other men, but only in degree' (169). This kind/degree distinction has a long pedigree in republican thought, reconciling a belief in equality under the law with a belief in the deference owed to natural leaders – men 'possessed of more than usual organic sensibility who had also thought long and deeply' (157).[17] Wordsworth shifts emphasis from the laws to the 'spirit' of the laws – to culture understood as what Raymond Williams describes as structures of feeling. If poetry is politics practiced by other means, we can appreciate not only Wordsworth's disdain for plays and novels, but his concern with the most 'dishonourable' charge that can be brought against a poet: that he has failed 'to ascertain what is his duty' (156). As Williams noted, the 'man speaking to men' formula speaks to the division of labour and fear of specialization.[18] It implies a dutiful disinterestedness not to be expected from labourers, artisans or women; it implies liberal education and contemplative leisure.

Wordsworth was not striving to 'overthrow the reigning tradition' of humanist education; he was striving to reconstitute it in the face of economic forces threatening to 'blunt the discriminating powers of the mind' (160). But there were other romantics who addressed the issue of 'culture' by siding with Edwin rather than the Hermit, most notably Joanna Baillie. Baillie's 1798 introduction to *A Series of Plays* is the democratic treatise on education that the preface to *Lyrical Ballads* is not. Women writers obviously stood in a different relation to humanism, imitation and virtue than did men. For one thing, untutored Shakespeare and not learned Spenser was the special object of their attention. Beattie dedicated the *Minstrel* to Elizabeth Montague, who had recently defended Shakespeare against Voltaire and the shackles of French criticism in *An Essay on the Writings and Genius of Shakespear* (1769). The example of Shakespeare leads Baillie, in marked contrast to Wordsworth, to favour the theatre as the preferred site of instruction: 'the impressions made by it are communicated, at the same instant of time, to a greater number of individuals, than those made by any other species of writing; and they are strengthened in every spectator, by observing their effects upon those who surround him' (58).[19] Baillie turns to 'our great national Dramatist' (26n) both as a model to imitate and as an authority for the argument that imitation is unnecessary and even harmful.

Like Beattie and Wordsworth, Baillie believes that 'strong passions . . . carry on a similar operation in the breast of the Monarch, and the man of low degree' (42); in the passions she discovers permanent 'principles in the human mind' (41) as opposed to 'adventitious distinctions amongst men, of age, fortune, rank, profession, and country' (53). Like Beattie (but unlike Wordsworth) she regards knowledge of the passions as immediate: 'a peasant will very clearly perceive in the character of a peer, those native peculiarities which belong to him as a man' (50). In Baillie's account, the education of the passions proceeds from 'sympathetic curiosity' (4): curiosity draws our empathy towards anyone different from us, empathy leads to sympathy, sympathy to the discovery in them of the laws informing our own human nature. As she most succinctly expresses the argument, 'In examining others we know ourselves' (12). Her sociology is at odds with discrimination, be it moral or aesthetic: with the example of Shakespeare before her, she can say that 'A decidedly wicked character can never be interesting; and to employ such for the display of any strong passion would very much injure instead of improving the moral effect' (65). Instead of locating aesthetic pleasure in the discovery of likeness in difference, she locates it in the discovery of likeness in similarity: 'The highest pleasures we receive from poetry, as well as from the real objects which surround us in the world, are derived from the sympathetick interest we all take in beings like ourselves' (23).

Baillie's belief that literature and society should be structured by common interests rather than uncommon virtue differentiates her otherwise similar arguments from Wordsworth's project for aesthetic education. As a democratic thinker, she is deeply suspicious of any disinterestedness founded on the belief that some people are better than others – in kind *or* degree. She quite properly identifies disinterestedness with humanist practices of imitation: the 'bold disinterested beings' of classical tragedy 'have been held forth to our view as objects of imitation and interest; as though they had entirely forgotten that it is only from creatures like ourselves that we feel, and therefore, only from creatures like ourselves that we receive the instruction of example' (34n, 33). She excoriates Greek drama for a lack 'of action and of passion' that would have made it 'more irregular, more imperfect, more varied, more interesting' (27–8). Sympathetic curiosity is more strongly aroused by untutored Shakespeare, who recognized the value of gross and violent stimulants.

The force of Baillie's nationalist appeal to Shakespeare should not be underestimated: at a time when radicals espousing similar view were being sent to prison, *Plays on the Passions* was almost universally admired. Nor should her appeal to 'common' interests be discounted, for Baillie's reputation was made when it was discovered that the author of this manly essay was a woman. Her fame created a larger public for women writers and established the role they were to play in educating a new kind of reader. In 1826, the Ettrick Shepherd, who made a career out of untutored genius, gave priority to the 'large and lustrous star o' Joanna Baillie' in a catalogue of women writers including Hamilton, Edgeworth, Grant, Austen, Tighe, Mitford and Hemans, whom he salutes as 'the union o' genius, and virtue, and religion, and morality, and gentleness, and purity . . . a soul uplifting sight [that] ratifies the great bond of Nature, by which we are made heirs of the immortal sky.'[20] As with Shakespeare, women's lack of formal training affirms the 'bond of nature'. In 1841, the *Quarterly Review* argued that Baillie's contribution to the 'reformation' of British literature was owing 'partly to the simplicity of a Scotch education, partly to the influence of the better portions of Burns' poetry, but chiefly to the spontaneous action of . . . forceful genius' in a poet 'unversed in the ancient languages and literatures'.[21]

The issues I have discussed were all revisited in American debates over literary education early in the twentieth century. Irving Babbitt, the neohumanist, followed Wordsworth in identifying commerce and sensationalism as besetting evils to be overcome by disciplined reflection on the permanent human concerns. Babbitt despised what he regarded as the fatuousness and amoralism of romantic philosophy. His opponent, Arthur Lovejoy, followed Coleridge's lead in subordinating poetry to epistemology; upholding German philology and historicism, he dismissed Babbitt as a lightweight: 'the more earnest the moralist, the more justly suspect the historian'. Lovejoy's model for the research university, like his interpretation of romanticism, triumphed utterly. It did so, however, in conjunction with a recuperation of Hazlitt's 'spirited' politics. Ernest Bernbaum's *Guide Through the Romantic Movement* imitates the *Spirit of the Age* in form and doctrine: Wordsworth 'sets no value upon distinctions of birth or rank or wealth; he has a deep, affectionate respect for the plain people; and the ideals and ways of life which he advocates can be followed by men and women in the humblest circumstances. . . Not to know and love Wordsworth is therefore to be out of harmony with the soul of our Anglo-American world.'[22]

The six-poet romanticism taught to American college students stems from the desire of progressive educators to bestow on British romanticism the intellectual pedigree of German philosophy and the political pedigree of French democracy.[23] In sober truth, this interpretation is no more partial than the romantic reading of the Renaissance: both were driven by the political and educational concerns of their place and time. But it has been brutal to writers who were Scottish, Irish or female. In presenting romanticism as revolution, *Norton* marginalizes Goldsmith, Burns, Scott and Moore, and altogether excludes Macpherson, Beattie and Burke. With 'liberal' education under attack from both the left and the right, with scholarly enquiry into the literary origins of nationalism underway, we can expect renewed attention to these authors and their feminine counterparts. ❦

Virginia Polytechnic Institute and State University

1 Robert Crawford, *Devolving English Literature* (Oxford: Clarendon, 1992) 3. The qualification is important, for verse had always been used in elementary instruction. The study of vernacular literature in dissenting academies and grammar schools increased throughout the eighteenth-century, as documented by John Lawson and Harold Silver, *A Social History of Education in England* (London: Methuen, 1973) 181–89 and Richard S. Tompson, *Classics or Charity? The Dilemma of the Eighteenth-Century Grammar School* (Manchester: Manchester University Press, 1971) 36–72. It was also taught at Oxford and Cambridge, though not as part of the formal curriculum. See Robert D. J. Palmer, *The Rise of English Studies: An Account of the Study of English Language and Literature From its Origins to the Making of the Oxford English School* (London: Oxford University Press, 1965) 1–14. See also Linda Colley, *Britons: Forging the Nation 1707–1837* (New Haven: Yale University Press, 1992) 11–17 and passim.

2 Relatively few histories of 'culture' have been written; the best of them remains Raymond Williams, *Culture and Society, 1780–1950* (London: Chatto and Windus, 1958). See also E. H. Gombrich, *In Search of Cultural History* (Oxford: Clarendon, 1969) and Karl J. Weintraub, *Visions of Culture* (Chicago, University of Chicago Press, 1966). These are 'cultural' histories of culture that beg the kinds of radical questions that need to be asked. I have tried to write a different kind of history in *Forms of Reflection: Genre and Culture in Meditational Writing* (Baltimore: Johns Hopkins University Press, 1993). On the Scottish contribution, see my essay 'Ossian and the Genres of Culture,' *Studies in Romanticism* 31 (1992) 213–32.

3 On the survival and adaptation of classical practices of imitation, see George Pigman, 'Imitation and the Renaissance sense of the Past: The Reception of Erasmus' Ciceronianus,' *Journal of Medieval and Renaissance Studies* 9 (1979) 155–77; and 'Versions of Imitation in the Renaissance,' *Renaissance Quarterly* 33 (1980) 1–32; Thomas M. Greene, *The Light in Troy: Imitation and Discovery in Renaissance Poetry* (New Haven: Yale University Press, 1981); on eighteenth-century practices of imitation, see Francis Galloway, *Reason, Rule, and Revolt in English Classicism* (New York: Scribners, 1940) 210–27; and Howard D. Weinbrot, ' "An Ambition to Excell": The Aesthetics of Emulation in the Seventeenth and Eighteenth Centuries,' *Huntington Library Quarterly* 48 (1985) 121–39. For the romantic period, see Greg Kucich, *Keats, Shelley, & Romantic Spenserianism* (University Park: Pennsylvania State University, 1991).

4 The status of women writers during the romantic era has been discussed by Mary Poovey, *The Proper Lady and the Woman Writer: Ideology as Style in the Works of Mary Wollstonecraft, Mary Shelley and Jane Austen* (Chicago, University of Chicago Press, 1984); Mary Jacobus, *Reading Woman: Essays in Feminist Criticism* (New York: Columbia University Press, 1986); Margaret Homans, *Women Writers and Poetic Identity: Dorothy Wordsworth, Emily Bronte, and Emily Dickinson* (Princeton: Princeton University Press, 1980), essays in Anne K. Mellor, ed. *Romanticism and Feminism* (Bloomington: Indiana University Press, 1988); Marlon B. Ross, *The Contours of Masculine Desire: Romanticism and the Rise of Women's Poetry* (New York: Oxford University Press, 1989).

5 On the reception, see Margaret S. Carhart, *The Life and Work of Joanna Baillie* (1923, rpt. New York: Archon, 1970) 14–68, passim.

6 M. H. Abrams, ed., *The Norton Anthology of English Literature*, 2 vols. (Fourth Edition; New York: Norton, 1979).

7 For romanticism as a Renaissance revival, see William Lyon Phelps, *The Beginnings of the English Romantic Movement* (Boston: Ginn, 1893); R. S. Crane, 'Imitation of Spenser and Milton in the Early Eighteenth Century,' *Studies in Philology* 15 (1918) 195–206; R. D. Havens, *The Influence of Milton on English Poetry* (Cambridge: Harvard University Press, 1922); Harko G. De Maar, *A History of Modern English Romanticism* (London: Oxford University Press, 1924);

Earl R. Wasserman, *Elizabethan Poetry in the Eighteenth Century* (Urbana: University of Illinois Press, 1947); Galloway, 259–75.

8 See Richard C. Frushell, 'Spenser and the Eighteenth-Century Schools,' *Spenser Studies* 7 (1986) 175–98.

9 *The Poetical Works of James Beattie*, ed. Alexander Dyce (London: Bell, 1894). Citations are by book and stanza.

10 Similar conceptions, of course, can be found in Blackwell's *An Enquiry into the Life and Writings of Homer* (London, 1735), Brown's *A Dissertation on the Rise, Union, and Power, the Progressions, Separations, and Corruptions, of Poetry and Music* (London, 1763), and Fergusson, *An Essay on Civil Society* (Dublin, 1763). These writers are discussed in Lois Whitney's classic essay in the 'history of ideas,' *Primitivism and the Idea of Progress in English Popular Literature of the Eighteenth Century* (Baltimore: Johns Hopkins, 1934).

11 William Dowling's valuable essay on mid-century poetry presents the Gothic revival as a modification of an earlier civic humanism, a modification that renders history as 'ideology': 'this is the context in which Bolingbroke's idealization of the Elizabethan age, for instance, and of Elizabeth herself as a monarch who "united the great body of the people in her and their *common interest*" must be seen as part of his more general idealization of organic society [involving] appeals to the Ancient Constitution, and in particular to what he calls England's Gothic institutions of government' 'Ideology in Eighteenth-Century Poetry', in Leo Damrosch, ed. *The Profession of Eighteenth-Century Literature: Reflections on an Institution* (Madison: University of Wisconsin Press, 1992) 139.

12 See Philip Doyne, *Irene, a Canto on the Peace; Written in the Stanza of Spenser* (1763); *The Triumph of Parnassus, a Poem on the Birth of His Royal Highness the Prince of Wales* (1763); John Ball, *Odes, Elegies, Ballads, Pictures, Inscriptions, Sonnets* (1772?); Samuel Whyte, ed. *The Shamrock: or Hibernian Cresses. A Collection of Poems, Songs, Epigrams, &c. Latin as well as English, the Original Production of Ireland* (1772); and the several volumes published by Thomas Dermody (1775–1803); James Bland Burgess, *The Birth and Triumph of Love* (1796), *Richard the First: a Poem in Eighteen Books*, 2 vols. (1801). As a boy, Edmund Burke is said to have read *The Faerie Queene* among the ruins of Kilcolman.

13 *The Letters of John Keats*, ed. Maurice Buxton Forman (third edition, London: Oxford University Press, 1947) 259.

14 In fact, Wordsworth echoes the taunts neoclassical writers hurled at 'romantic' writers, such as Lloyd in 'The Poetry Professors': 'Whilom, what time, eftsoons and erst, / (So prose is oftentimes beverst) / Sprinkled with quaint fantastic phrase, / Uncouth to ears of modern days,' (Works, 1774), or Johnson: 'If there be, what I believe there is in every nation, a style so consonant and congenial . . . as to remain settled and unaltered; this style is probably to be sought in the common intercourse of life, among those who speak to be understood, without ambition of elegance. The polite are always catching modish speech in hope of finding or making better; those who wish for distinction forsake the vulgar, when the vulgar is right' *Johnson on Shakespeare*, ed. H. R. Woudhuysen (London: Penguin, 1989) 128.

15 References, by page number, are to *Lyrical Ballads*, ed. W. J. B. Owen (Oxford: Oxford University Press, 1969).

16 *The Critical Opinions of William Wordsworth*, ed. Markham L. Peacock, Jr. (Baltimore: Johns Hopkins, 1950) 183.

17 As J. G. A. Pococke summarizes the argument, 'At all events, though the many acknowledge the few to be superior in their capacities, the relation between debate and result is one of equality. Deference, then, is perfectly compatible with equality, so long as the latter is

proportionate equality in the Aristotelian sense. Indeed, this sort of equality cannot exist unless qualitative distinctions and inequalities among men are recognized' 'The Classical Theory of Deference,' *American Historical Review* 81:3 (1976) 518.

18 Williams, 39–47. See also John Barrell's account of the relation of disinterested virtue to professional specialization in *The Political Theory of Painting from Reynolds to Hazlitt* (New Haven: Yale University Press, 1986) 1–68.

19 Baillie, *A Series of Plays: In Which it is attempted to Delineate the Stronger Passions of the Mind*, facsimile, ed. Donald H. Reiman (New York: Garland, 1977).

20 Reprinted in Wilson, *Noctes Ambrosianae* (Edinburgh: Blackwood, 1887) 1:271. The sentiments may be Wilson's rather than Hogg's.

21 Quoted in Carhart, 76.

22 See Irving Babbitt, *Literature and the American College* (1908; rpt. Chicago: Gateway, 1956); Arthur O. Lovejoy, review of *Rousseau and Romanticism*, MLN 25 (1920) 308; Ernest Bernbaum, *Guide Through the Romantic Movement*, 2 vols. (New York: Nelson, 1930) 1:144, 151.

23 Bernbaum's progressive politics are admirably overt, as is his contempt for 'preromanticism': 'confused, disassociated, and illogical', 1:18. Compare Bernbaum's views (codified in *Norton*) to earlier textbooks, where Burns is the prince of poets, Burke of rhetoricians, and Scott of novelists. See, for example, Charles D. Cleveland, *A Compendium of English Literature* (Philadelphia, 1868) or Truman J. Backus, *Shaw's New History of English Literature* (New York: Sheldon and Company, 1875, 1884).

JOHN PURSER

The canonicity of Scottish music

When Programme 17 of BBC Radio Scotland's series *Scotland's Music* won the gold medal at the Sony Awards in 1993 for best specialist music programme, its competitors in the final were Classic FM and Radio 3. And what did the band play as Martin Dalby and I went up to collect our awards and blink at the cameras? They played *Scotland the Brave*.

The fact that Programme 17 consisted entirely of 18th century compositions by James Oswald did not render the bandleader's choice wholly irrelevant, for Oswald was a musical patriot for his country and had fond memories of 'Hieland heather' and the like: but it did cause Martin and me to exchange glances of wry humour, though both knowing only too well that had the band been playing in Glasgow as opposed to London they would probably have come up with much the same choice.

So there we are. The canonicity of Scottish music is defined in the world publicity stakes by the image of tartan and heather which fondly survives from the days of the music hall and is as indestructible as *The Scots Magazine*. Nor do I wish to destroy this music in this article. It is popular, it does little injury to anyone, and it gives great pleasure to thousands, the world over. What I do wish to destroy is the aural image of Scotland which cannot hear anything else coming from it.

There is of course an international audience for Scottish traditional music of various kinds, and within each grouping there is an accepted canon. For piobaireachd lovers *The Lament for the Children* is sacred, and it is only recently that the predominance of the MacCrimmons has been counteracted by the MacDonalds, and that the *Kilberry Book of Ceol Mor* has been challenged as a source. Thomason's work still remains to be restored to its proper prominence, and such is the strength of canonicity in the competition world that manifest distortions of rhythm and melody have become *de rigeur*, in much the same way as well-known opera singers hang hopefully on to their top notes, in search of brute applause.

In the world of the ballad singers, there is, of course, the great canon of the Child ballads, matched melodically by Bronson's collection of the tunes. But, because ballads are part of an oral tradition not dependent on competition, the canon can be challenged. But it is not my aim to enter into the niceties of performance practice, or to delve into the rich disputes and varied renderings of material in the world of tradition. Suffice it to say that there are orthodoxies and there are challengers.

The real challenge has come with respect to the canonicity of Scottish classical music. Let us look at the critical history of the man now widely regarded as Scotland's greatest composer – Robert Carver. Incredibly, outside his own music manuscript, there is no mention of him as a composer in any century (including his own) until this one, in which, until recently, it was distinctly mixed. Even Kenneth Elliott, who has done so much for Carver's reputation, has been very cautious in his claims, having to bear the torch alone against the lukewarm condescensions of the leading English musicologist, Frank Harrison. The fact that Harrison cannot have had anything more than a superficial knowledge of Carver's music, and manifestly knew nothing of its cultural background and could have heard only a tiny proportion of it, did not prevent him from treating Carver as a kind of forward provincial, meriting only a paragraph. In fact a Hungarian, Gabor Darvas, was one of the first to treat Carver with respect, though poor Henry George Farmer had, in earlier days, been desperately trying to discover what the music sounded like by arranging it for his theatre band to play as entre-acte music, despairing of ever getting together a suitable choir for it! This story was told me in a letter by an ex-professor of music at Glasgow University who, over many years, had it in his power to do something for Carver. He seemed to see no irony in recounting this tale, oblivious, apparently, to the appalling indictment of his own stewardship.

So where was Carver in the canon of Scottish classical composers? He was nowhere. But that was no great stigma as there was not even such a thing as a canon, such was the lack of research. Carver is now widely accepted as a composer of genius and immense technical variety and expertise, with an extraordinary command of vocal sonority, finally revealed in splendid recordings by the Tavener Singers and by Cappella Nova, which latter have recorded all Carver's surviving works.

Let us look at other leading figures. Kenneth Elliott has again done much for Robert Johnson and for William Kinloch. But most of Johnson's music is unpublished, and this is also true of Kinloch, whose two major works (the Pasmessour and Quadrant Pavans with their respective Galliards) received their first modern performances only at the recording session for a CD issued in the spring of 1993. I had not had time to transcribe them when I wrote my book, having already had to transcribe two other major works of his to get them their first broadcasts and a first modern performance. Now it is an exciting business to be responsible for making music available that has been locked away for centuries, but it is simply disgraceful that it has not been available hitherto, and I am deeply conscious of the fact that my discussion of Kinloch is now grossly inadequate, simply because the material was not available and there was a limit to what I could achieve in the time.

The reader may now be questioning on what basis I am putting forward these works for inclusion in a canon. The answer is simple. We have little enough surviving and there is therefore rarely any need to push out one composer because another is somehow to be preferred. If you want to listen to Scottish music for keyboard from the turn of the 16th-17th centuries, there is Kinloch, a few works ascribed to Burnett or anonymous, and that is it. If the music has any merit, our musical history has room for it. It is my opinion that it is very fine music indeed, worthy of international recognition, but we are not in the luxurious position of having to juggle with several such claimants.

In these circumstances, it is beyond comprehension that a manuscript such as the Sprouston Breviary (one of only a handful of mediaeval music manuscripts with Scottish material in them) should have gone so long untranscribed; or that the only serious research work done on many aspects of Scottish music has been undertaken by Americans such as Edward Roesner and Ann Germain. The Balcarres lute book has been transcribed by an Englishman, Matthew Spring. The Scottish lute repertoire is recorded by a Swede (Jakob Lindberg) and an American (Ronn MacFarlane). The American Baltimore Ensemble have transcribed and recorded much Scottish music otherwise unheard.

There have, of course, been Scottish contributions from the Scottish Early Music Consort and Cappella Nova (both run by English couples) and the work of Kenneth Elliott and David Johnson has been seminal. But it is still possible to buy a score of only one work of Sir John Clerk, so it is very difficult to arrange for performances. Most of Oswald's music is unpublished. Only recently have a couple of works of McGibbon become available. Kelly is again only represented by four or five works in print or on record. MacKenzie is extremely hard to get, and in several works (as with MacCunn's opera, *Jeannie Deans*), has had to have a complete set of parts reconstructed from the score. Thomson is virtually entirely in manuscript (I have transcribed three works to make them legible for performance, and one of his piano trios has no full score); and I have spent a small fortune in time and photocopying sending people material which they simply cannot otherwise obtain.

One of the major problems, then, is the lack of research, published editions, and recordings. Another is the outrageous failure of our education system at all levels to make our children and students aware of the history of the nation they are privileged to live in. To establish a Scottish canon in any discipline you have to actually know what it is to be Scottish. Few do, and the Scots themselves must bear much of the blame. Perhaps the two single most influential people in the development of the study of Scottish history as a respectable as well as fascinating subject are Smout and Prebble. They are both Englishmen. On the music side, Henry George Farmer was an Irishman, and such credit as I may take to myself relates to the fact that I too am Irish, although wholly resident and educated in Scotland. I had knowledge of the culture of Ireland and I knew that it had self-respect, and I saw no reason why the same should not be true for Scotland. I was not brought up with the depressed self-assessment of the citizen of a colonially-driven culture whose Queen implicitly denies her own status as monarch by deliberately flying the English royal standard over Holyrood House, though it has been made clear to her that it causes offence and that she should be flying the Scottish royal standard.

Never has that culture been more colonially driven than now. Our 'representation' in Parliament is a manifest mockery, full of gerrymandering, and resembling true democracy no more closely than our Secretary of State represents the nation he is supposed to serve. In such circumstances it should not have surprised me, when lecturing trainee primary school teachers, that I was only able to get through to them when I devoted the first thirty minutes of my talk to a potted history of Scotland so that they actually had some inkling of major events such as Flodden, the Unions of the Crowns and Parliaments, and so on. That history was welcome to them. At last they had a context in which to understand what they heard, but it should not fall to an outside lecturer on Scottish music to fill that staggering gap.

The self-doubt of the Scots is still manifesting itself. The series of concerts of Scottish music at the Edinburgh International Festival of 1992 was a great success, with audiences, on BBC Radio 3, and with visitors from abroad. But the Scottish critics made no attempt to study unfamiliar works in advance, and matched their ignorance with caution and downright idiocy. James Oswald, who rose to be Chamber composer to George III and who had long since had entries as a composer as well as publisher in all major music dictionaries (the best in *Musik in Geschichte und Gegenwart*, which is rather better than Groves) was described by Raymond Monelle as 'not really a composer at all', and Michael Tumelty had nothing to say about him other than to refer to two 'batty cantatas', omitting to inform his readers that they are satirical works. Yet, as I pointed out at the beginning of this article, the Sony Gold award went to a programme lasting 90 minutes which was entirely devoted to the music of James Oswald. People do not give awards for programmes featuring music unworthy of attention.

Here are other examples. The first modern recordings of orchestral works by MacKenzie and McEwen have been made by English orchestras. Why not the Scottish National Orchestra, or the BBC Scottish Symphony Orchestra? The first performances of several McEwen chamber works I have known of in my lifetime were given in the Van Gogh Museum in Amsterdam in January 1993, to accompany the Glasgow 1900 exhibition. They were very warmly received. And when the BBCSSO performed MacKenzie's Violin Concerto, the soloist, Mi-Kyung Lee, could not understand how such lovely music could be so long neglected. Yet James MacMillan, perhaps under too much obligation to his own radicalism, basically dismissed MacKenzie as a non-starter, and Conrad Wilson described Thomson's Piano Trio and MacKenzie's magnificent Piano Quartet as 'no more than a ragbag of echoes'. Now such remarks are born of profound ignorance of the date and history of these works. The Thomson Trio was admired by Mendelssohn, and the MacKenzie Piano Quartet (published in Leipzig) so impressed Hans von Bulow that he sought out MacKenzie in Edinburgh and subsequently performed the work. These were, in their respective periods, two of the finest musicians alive and it is inconceivable that they would approve of works which were 'a ragbag of echoes', a matter on which they would have been extremely well informed.

The tragedy is that one has to go back a century and a half, to distinguished foreigners, to actually get an informed opinion on these pieces. Our academics have offered no serious analysis of them, publish no critical magazine on matters related to Scottish music, and produce very very few articles for music magazines; and our music critics seem more concerned with populism than developing a knowledge and vocabulary suitable to the matter which they mention rather than discuss. In the case of MacKenzie other vile prejudices enter the field. In some circles it is still unrespectable to think highly of the late 19th century unless it is Wagner. Even Brahms is given the thumbs down and anything resembling comfort and happiness of the Dickensian sort are not considered good enough for music unless they make it very clear to you that they are the children of agony. What monstrous aesthetic sentimentalism! But it is propagated by the very people who are looking for sentimentalism under every bush so they can flush it out and make it shiver.

But there is another problem for the Scots in particular, namely, who is a Scot? We cannot expect foreigners, least of all those of the English variety, to go sniffing around and identifying Scots when it saves so much trouble to call them all English anyway. Hence it is that Tobias Hume, who was obviously by name and trade a Scot (he was a mercenary in Sweden, Russia and Poland in the late 16th century), has been hitherto credited as English because he published and died in England. Nobody has yet been able to discover when and where he was born. I risked all in giving a substantial place to him in my 'canon', and was rewarded some months after publication with the emergence of a transcript of Queen Anne's papers in which Hume, on his first appearance, is described as 'the Scottish musician'. So what? Well, Hume was a pioneer in the development of the viola da gamba, and some of his compositions are not only very fine, but also include the earliest examples of a variety of techniques. Where did he acquire this skill and daring? While he was soldiering? It is possible. But now we must take seriously the possibility that he was the product of a developed school of viol playing in Scotland, such as might have been sustained by the Hudson family of violers, themselves imported from England by James VI.

And what if it turns out that Walter Frye is a Scot? Apart from anything else it would provide us with the only music from the 15th century by a named composer. But the identification rests only on the fact that a part of a composition of his on a fresco in France is traditionally said to have been composed by a Scottish monk. We have nothing else on Frye's origins, but who, if anybody, has been seriously looking for him north of the border?

So if people want to make a fuss about canonicity, let them remember that they can only do so from the position of existing knowledge and choice. The great thing is to steer clear of the living. If you have a favourite you want to write about in your canon, for goodness sake have him or her removed from this vale of tears as rapidly as possible so that the rivals for favour have lost half of their motivation. After all, one does not want to become part of the canon oneself by an unnecessary martyrdom. But it is my view that it is open to anyone with energy to establish the canon for themselves. The problem of canonicity only really arises when people have for too long been too lazy to question their teachers. 🍎

Glasgow

DUNCAN MACMILLAN

The canon in Scottish art : Scottish art in the canon

The idea of the canon in this post-structuralist era is problematic in any discipline, but in art, where much of the creative effort of recent times has been directed at the destruction of just such hierarchic concepts, it is perhaps the least appropriate. The Futurists, for instance, right at the beginning of this century, proposed the destruction of the art galleries of Italy because they enshrine such ideas. They were following in the age-old tradition of icono-clasm in which canonical ideas of any kind are identified as obstacles to freedom, a tradition whose misunderstood heritage has been the black dog of Scottish art history. Alternatively, one of the greatest modern Scottish artists, Eduardo Paolozzi, originally based his art on the idea that the notion of fine art itself, a category that depends on the unspoken assumptions of the canon, is a mistake which cuts us off from the vitality in our own culture and the true function of art. In one sense, therefore, to speak of a Scottish canon at all is to be disloyal to the tradition that bore us.

Nevertheless, it is worth examining the idea of the canon, as it is surely the case that there is such a thing and that it plays a part in many of our assumptions about European art. Anybody could identify its main outlines; such ideas as the primacy in the art of Europe, first of the Italian Renaissance and then later of France, or the central place of the masters of modernism like Picasso and Matisse in any account of the twentieth century, all stand unquestioned. They are assumptions that underlie most general commentary on western civilisation and, although much scholarship nowadays may fall outside of these canonical limits, they too often still shape the thinking of scholars wherever they may focus their attention, just as much as they shape the assumptions of the non-professional. The place where they are made explicit and are most familiar, however, is in the great art galleries. The major British and American galleries, the National Gallery in London, or the Metropolitan in New York, for instance, are deliberately canonical in their organisation and in their objectives.

In the National Gallery in London a coherent and very impressive collection of British art is on display in the main run of the galleries, but only that part of the British, or more accurately the English tradition, is included which is held to be canonical in European terms, roughly from Hogarth to Turner. Ramsay, Raeburn and Wilkie, though they belong chronologically, are not represented. The Tate Gallery, which has a very muddled brief, holds the main collection of national art which by implication, because it is apart from the *National* Gallery and the *international* canon that it presents, is non-canonical in European terms, just as the putative gallery of Scottish art would also be. In fact the Tate Gallery's British collection – the national collection of British Art – represents a chronicle not a canon. It tells a story. It does not present simply the 'best of British' selection, which is seen as the National Gallery's job, though with the important reservation noted above, that the British school only has a limited and particular place in the international canon.

In France in the Musée d'Orsay an attempt has been made to move away from the conventional canonical structure. The collections have been arranged as a chronicle on quasi-structuralist lines. (Although the visitor might be forgiven for supposing it is a gallery of French art, it does in fact have an international brief.) It is structuralist in the way that the whole story of nineteenth-century art has been hung together. Thus the 'pompiers' (the inflated academic works) are hung along with the radicals. Questions of preference based on taste or the canonical status of individual works are unimportant in the presentation of the wider structure that it is proposed will be thus revealed. The effect, though, is actually to weaken the impact of the whole, for the dramatically radical vision of the great painters of the late nineteenth century is diluted in the conservatism of the pompiers. It is drained of its significance by being brought down to their level.

But what of a Scottish canon and its place in this wider European canon? We might expect to find the answer to this question in the National Gallery of Scotland, but though many of the works that should form part of this Scottish canon do in fact belong to the nation, they are not presented in a way that answers this question. That this is so is illuminating of the way the accepted canon works. The National Gallery is in fact exactly the opposite of what its title suggests. It is called the *National* Gallery, but it is the gallery in which the *international* canon can be seen, laid out by schools and chronology, and it is exclusive. Scottish art is only tacked on in a way that suggests, at the very least, that these questions have not been addressed, let alone resolved. (In Glasgow a bold experiment to break with the canon has been made and Kelvingrove rehung along non-canonical lines, but the merit of such a radical departure is rather spoiled by the cynically opportunistic attempt being made by Glasgow at the same time to capture the proposed new gallery of Scottish art, thus endorsing the worst effect of the application of the canonical idea, the separation (by real physical distance in this case) and demotion of the national art because it is outside the canon.)

The same is true of the Scottish National Gallery of Modern Art. There is a modern canon which significantly is distinct from the classic canon of art history, though it is just as institutionalised. As a consequence, the SNGMA has adopted as its objective, not the role foreseen it originally by Cursiter when he first proposed such an institution, as a kind of powerhouse for art in Scotland, but as a passive repository for works that could represent this modernist international canon. There is a fine Scottish collection, although as the exhibition a few years ago, *Scottish Art Since 1900*,[1] made clear, it has not been built up consistently, it is far from comprehensive and its development and display seem always to have taken second place.

The case of the National Galleries of Scotland reveals how, although art is not subdivided by the boundaries of language as literature is, the art canon is nevertheless defined geographically. Some art is included by definition, other art can never be. Excluding the conspicuous success of the Scottish National Portrait Gallery as a national institution, the National Gallery of Scotland is otherwise wedded to the international canon, in which according to these geographical rules, Scotland has no place. The proposed Gallery of Scottish art, on the other hand, will either have no coherence, or it will move the best of the nation's art out of the national collection altogether. Such a proposal marginalises the Scottish tradition, suggesting that we cannot see ourselves as having a claim to be paid-up members of Europe, but instead that we are second-class citizens, dependent on other cultures for the values by which we live. This certainly expresses a negative political attitude in the immediate context of Scottish politics, but it also reflects a more universal negation, for it denies the social function of the nation's art and distorts our whole understanding of the role of art. It also reveals our national art collections as instruments of power, as devices for the manipulation of the nation's self-perception. The creation of a separate modern canon has the same effect though with a much wider relevance, for it cuts modern art off from its root in Western radical thought, thus depriving it of a vital source of nourishment and the natural strength that comes from continuity.

The issue of the Scottish canon and whether or not it exists, or can exist, is inextricably bound up with the question of its place in the wider European canon. By the same token, to attempt to define it in isolation would immediately diminish it into provincialism as a separate Scottish gallery threatens to do. Before its relationship to the wider canon can be discussed, it must nevertheless first be outlined.

The period which defined the central achievement of Scottish art was the period that also defined the central achievement in Scottish thought, the Enlightenment. Its relationship in turn to the central event in Scottish history, the Reformation, remains an open question, however. Indeed it is one of the greatest questions that face Scottish intellectual history. It already has a bearing on it, however, that the first canonical image in modern Scottish art, George Jamesone's *Self-Portrait at an Easel* (c. 1644) dates virtually from the period of the Reformation and long before any conventional dating of the Enlightenment. In this picture, we are addressed directly by a self-conscious, professional artist. He is using his art in the service of society, but, as he does so, along with the indications of his trade and his status, by the device of a picture within a picture which represents the chastisement of Cupid – the senses put in their place – and the still-life of 'vanitas' and 'memento mori' imagery, he reminds us of the presence in any simple representation of the unspoken metaphysical questions; of the tension between the physical description and the metaphysical presence that it implies, but which, bound by the rules of empirical perception, it can never describe.

Jamesone had thus already set an agenda that stood for painting for at least the succeeding one hundred and fifty years, but it was not till the first years of the following century that the art of native born Scots evolved again to a position where they could follow it. William Aikman and John Smibert took a position as painters that was, like that of Jamesone, essentially Anglo-Dutch, but they applied to it the lessons of Italian art, lessons about dignity and formality which strengthened their vision of individuality without clouding it, just as their contemporaries, James Smith, Colen Campbell and James Thomson, drew on the classical traditions in architecture and poetry but to create a Scottish style. It is surely also significant that Smibert would also be bound to take his place in any canon of American painting.

Allan Ramsay inherited this position and the ambition to create an absolutely truthful image of the individual. But he incorporated into it more and more as his art evolved a sense of the wider order in which the individual belongs as a member of society – properly understood as the human environment. Ramsay's art is social just as his friend Hume's philosophy is. He recognises and indeed demonstrates how a proper understanding of each individual, as it necessarily deploys the imagination, is in a sense metaphysical and, therefore, how society itself depends on the dimension of metaphysical understanding that this represents. These ideas are enshrined in such images as *Lord Drummore* (1754), or indeed the second portrait of Hume himself (1766), but the canonical image here is surely Ramsay's portrait of his second wife, *Margaret Lindsay*, arranging flowers (c. 1758–60). As she turns with an open expression, thus identifying for us her intimacy with the painter, her husband, the painter's own skill in describing this identifies for us, through this particular and personal image, how, universally, human love depends on truth and on sympathy and the imagination that makes it possible.

With Raeburn this process is even further foreshortened so that in his portraits we see people intuitively, just as we experience them socially. Society is the given within which such images function. In his great painting of *Sir John and Lady Clerk of Penicuik* (1792) the sitters may be members of the landlord class and painted on a grand scale, but as Raeburn represents them this information is unimportant. They are above all a couple united by gentle affection, but their enclosure with each other does not set them apart from us. We see how it is only an extension and a deepening of the bonds of sympathy, the cement of society, that should unite us all.

Such images of course parallel closely how Hume and Adam Smith saw society and the human nature that composes it, but one of the central propositions of the Calvinist faith, the identification in communion of the metaphysical in the social community of equals, could also be seen in this light. Wilkie endeavoured to express this in his great, unfinished picture, *Knox Administering the Sacrament at Calder House* (begun c. 1839), a picture which stresses the social unity expressed in the communion. In his own words, he intended it to show how in the sacrament 'gentle and semple' – and also men and women – were present as equals.

It was, however, in *The Cotter's Saturday Night* (1837) that Wilkie gave the fullest account of this vision of society, both in the humanity of the Enlightenment version and in its original spiritual form. It is a picture in which the metaphysical proposition at the heart of this Calvinist/Enlightenment ideal is explicitly stated and it is the highest and most complete expression of this project that links the Enlightenment to the Reformation. It is perhaps therefore *the* canonical image of Scottish art. It is in the fullest sense a social picture, yet, without leaving that reality, the gentle sociability of a family gathered round the fire on a Saturday night is lifted towards the transcendental by the simple act of piety in which they are joined. It is a picture that owes a specific debt to Rembrandt, as Wilkie would have been proud to acknowledge, but the comparison also illuminates the difference. Rembrandt would have focussed such an image in the drama, even if it is the brilliant description of an unstated, internal drama as in his *Bathsheba*, but here there is no drama. Equally, the simple image of sociability that Wilkie creates is found in the work of Dutch painters like Steen and Ostade whom he also greatly admired, but they too seem to have felt the need to give some ulterior point to the sociability of their pictures and so they use humour where Rembrandt employed drama. For Wilkie, though, the simple human facts are enough without any such gloss or emphasis. The closest parallel is perhaps not in Dutch painting at all, but in those works of the Le Nains in which somehow, in just the same way, the most basic and unadorned social reality is invested with the mystery of the sacramental.

The picture of course takes its text from Burns and the imaginative force of its simplicity reflects Wilkie's awareness of another part of the agenda that painting shared with other branches of Scottish thought. One of the most significant features of the whole Enlightenment project was, as Ramsay and Raeburn both illustrated it, the proposal to incorporate the imagination into the structural functioning of society as the agent of the metaphysical bonds that unite it. This was the implicit burden of Smith's *Theory of Moral Sentiments* and Adam Fergusson and Hugh Blair related it directly to the freedom of the imagination in primitive society as it is revealed by primitive poetry, music, or indeed religion. In the 'Cotter's Saturday Night' Burns attributes just such simplicity of expression to the worship that he describes:

> They chant their artless notes in simple guise;
> They tune their hearts, by far the noblest aim . . .

As he does this, Burns makes an explicit association between an art form, music in this case, simplicity of expression and the idea of religious and therefore also implicitly moral purity. This has been one of the most potent ideas in modern art and it finds its earliest expression in the art of Gavin Hamilton. Blair and Fergusson were anticipated by Thomas Blackwell and Hamilton's Trojan pictures take their text almost as much from Blackwell and his pupil George Turnbull as from Homer himself,[2] but Hamilton was also with Adam Smith as a pupil of Francis Hutcheson. His links with Enlightenment thought are therefore many-stranded and direct and from his base in Rome Hamilton made these ideas available to European painters. His influence in France, for instance, and especially on J.-L. David, painter-hero of the French Revolution, is far more important than has been acknowledged hitherto.[3] To a large extent this is because of the way that the assumptions of the canon that have shaped scholarly writing presume the primacy of the French artist. Hamilton's painting of the *Death of Lucretia* is accepted as the model for David's key picture and one of the canonical images of modern art, *The Oath of the Horatii*, but what has not been previously recognised is how in his picture Hamilton is proposing a view of history more radical than David himself. In his picture, he presents an idea of sympathy that parallels Adam Smith's, because it is Lucretia who is the hero. He shows how her specifically feminine set of values and the action followed from them provoked the overthrow of the Tarquins.[4] Interestingly enough, following another of the unspoken assumptions of the canon, modern scholars have also altered Hamilton's title to give the leading role in the picture to the man. It has been known until recently, not by Hamilton's title, *The Death of Lucretia*, but as *The Oath of Brutus*.

It was among his Scottish followers that Hamilton's influence was most immediate and radical, however. The drawing of *Ossian Singing* that Alexander Runciman made in Rome in 1770 or 1771, deliberately free in execution and ignoring the niceties of accuracy and finish in the interest of expressive spontaneity, has a claim to be one of the earliest works of modern art. If Runciman's *Hall of Ossian* (1772) at Penicuik House had survived then that claim would be more widely recognised, for these paintings, destroyed by fire in 1899, were described by David Laing as 'truly national designs'.[5]

Ossian may be compromised as literature, but the influence of Macpherson's poetry on the visual arts needs no qualification. Significantly, in this drawing Runciman's Ossian is a musician and his music is the music of nature herself as the wind blows through the strings of his harp. The link between such imagery and the origins of the idea of a national landscape is direct. In the *Hall of Ossian* landscape played an important part and at Blair Castle, in a series of paintings of the waterfalls of Atholl, Runciman's contemporary, Charles Steuart, created the first images in the tradition of the celebration of the poetry invested in the Scottish landscape that continues to this day.

Another contemporary of Runciman, David Allan, though less of an artist, was also precocious in this respect. He collaborated with Burns, illustrating his Scots songs. George Thomson was the intermediary and Burns thought Allan's illustrations caught the quality of the songs very well.[6] Allan's illustrations to Allan Ramsay's *The Gentle Shepherd* also express these feelings, but it is perhaps his *Penny Wedding* that is Allan's most important contribution to the canon as it combines these qualities with a social ideal of harmony expressed in the primitive simplicity of folk music and dance. As it does so, it looks back through the Highland Wedding painted by Jacob de Wet, a Dutch artist working in Scotland in the late seventeenth century, to Breughel, but also, poetically, through Allan Ramsay to the older poetic tradition of Scotland. Raeburn took up this theme and focussed it even more intensely in his outstanding portrait of *Neil Gow* (c. 1793). Matching Burns's sentiment, Gow's fiddle playing too was famous for its artlessness, and Raeburn brilliantly matches its intuitive strength in the strength of his painting.

The integration and harmony that Raeburn captures in this painting expresses this side of the ambitions of the Enlightenment project. In a different way, in his two classic images of Edinburgh, Raeburn's friend Nasmyth sought to express the same idea of harmony. Together they constitute a vision of the just society. In the one, *Princes Street with the Building of the Royal Institution* (1825), the city is at work. In the foreground it is orchestrated by the architect, demonstrating the central place of art in society, for the building whose construction he is supervising, now the Royal Scottish Academy, is literally at the central point of the city. In the other, *Edinburgh from Calton Hill* (1825), the citizens' well-earned leisure is orchestrated by the philosopher, even from his tomb, for Hume's tomb is on the central axis of the picture. But such apparent harmony was bound to be illusory. Its central weakness, so devastatingly analysed by Marx, was that the society that such men as Nasmyth, radical friend of Burns, sought to unify was already irredeemably split by a fissure that only grew more profound as the Enlightenment progressed.

Even as Edinburgh's New Town was being built, the greatest monument to this vision of a society illuminated by knowledge, the seeds of alienation were already sown and its social base was too narrow to fulfil the ideals that it enshrines. As the truth of this became increasingly apparent, with the advance, hand-in-hand, of the Agricultural and Industrial Revolutions, as John Galt for instance so subtly describes it in *Annals of the Parish*, it was logical that thinking Scots should do as they did and, led by the likes of Wilkie and Chalmers, seek to renew the spiritual investment from which the whole project of a 'metaphysical' society had evolved. In the long and tangled series of events that led to the Disruption, the idea of this distinctively Scottish vision of society was one of the underlying constants.

It was Wilkie again who gave this definitive expression. He did this first in the *Letter of Introduction* (1813). There he expresses, through an image of the most inconsequential social encounter, the whole dilemma of the confrontation between the innocence of Enlightenment enthusiasm and the bitter facts of human experience, with a sub-text too of the confrontation of his own art, enshrining the Scottish tradition of social metaphysics, and his uncomprehending English audience. Then in the two pictures, *Distraining for Rent* (1815) and *The Penny Wedding* (1818), he formulated the anxieties that were in the end to frame the Disruption almost thirty years later. The two pictures respectively represent and thus oppose the old vision of a human order of society, united in harmony by music and dance, and the new order of alienation and social dislocation, the explicit failure of sympathy under the rule of law and profit. In the first picture, too, he consciously pays homage to two canonical images of Scottish art, Allan's *Penny Wedding* and Raeburn's *Neil Gow*. In the second, he pays homage to Hogarth whose own radical art had been marginalised in England by the academic reaction led by Reynolds.

This is not the place to pass judgment on the success or failure of the Disruption. To the extent that some at least of the ideals for which the seceders stood were expressed by Wilkie in the series of pictures which must stand near the centre of any canon of Scottish achievement in all the arts, however, that event must be seen, not as an attempt to turn the clock back, but as the expression of a precocious awareness of the spiritual and moral gap that was opening at the heart of modern society.

The compound of intellectual and spiritual anxieties that were part of this equation was given memorable expression by Dyce in one of the most beautiful paintings of the mid-century, *Pegwell Bay: a Recollection of October 5th 1858* (c. 1860). The date refers to the comet in the sky which invokes astronomical time. Geological time is invoked by the conspicuous stratifications of the rock in the cliffs in the background and at their feet, in the inexorable movement of the tide that over the millennia has shaped them. In contrast to these immensities, Dyce's sense of the pygmy scale of humanity is touchingly represented by the figures of his own family in the foreground.

It was, however, perhaps only a Highlander who could give complete expression to the tragic failure of the dream of a society united by sympathy, a dream which was perhaps just sustainable in a prosperous Lowland society, but which must always have seemed a delusion for the Highland people. In his painting of *The Emigrant Ship* (1895), William McTaggart, by birth a Gaelic speaker from the Mull of Kintyre, gave this fragmentation graphic expression as the scattered remnants of a displaced people dissolve into the landscape and the land itself dissolves into a stormy and uncertain sea. If Wilkie's *The Cotter's Saturday Night* encapsulates the humane idealism of the Enlightenment, McTaggart with the same economy summarises the forces that shattered it and which bore the modern world.

McTaggart's *Emigrant Ship* was painted almost one hundred years ago, yet it can still speak directly to us in the late twentieth century. The freedom with which he constructs the image in his work is not only a reflection, as here, of the violence underlying the scene he portrays, it is also a way of conveying the intuitive and irreducible subjectivity of the modern vision of the world. The Enlightenment's metaphysical vision of society had perhaps been an attempt to escape or at least compensate for the solipsism of this perception, but with McTaggart we already glimpse a very different solution made familiar by painters of the mid-twentieth century, the dissolution of self in the action which unites the painter with what he describes. Among the Scots, this is seen in the later work of William Johnstone and in the sea-scapes of Joan Eardley.

Amongst McTaggart's contemporaries, James Guthrie in the *Hind's Daughter* (1883) focuses for us a powerful motive behind the rural images favoured by late nineteenth-century artists: the fact that there are two sides to the process of alienation. From the picture, the girl looks out at the artist and at us with a detached indifference that shows her calm awareness of the social distance between us and how she inhabits a world of labour that, bourgeois like the artist, we cannot enter. In this situation, lesser painters, even Guthrie's model for this type of image, Bastien Lepage, fudged the issue by investing their subjects with endearing qualities and thus, with a blurring wash of spurious feeling, allow us to seem to bridge this gap. In its honesty and humanity and its clear recognition of social change, Guthrie's picture takes its place alongside Wilkie's and Raeburn's.

Guthrie's awareness was paralleled in the contemporary attempt by Patrick Geddes to find a new, secular solution to the division of society. In so doing, he still followed in outline the original Calvinist project of a society united by its highest function, not its lowest common denominator. If this also echoed Ruskin, it is perhaps an indication of how Ruskin's own thought was partly shaped both directly and indirectly by Scottish models. Geddes's own influence on Scottish culture generally has been far-reaching, however. In the visual arts, his direct initiatives included the encouragement of mural painting as a social form of art not compromised by market values. The outstanding artist here was Phoebe Traquair, the first major woman artist in Britain. Amongst her projects the decoration of the St Mary's Song School is the finest. It is perhaps partly because of Geddes, too, that a sense of the social responsibility of art has been kept alive by some of the greatest of our twentieth-century artists, first of all by Muirhead Bone in his war drawings, notably too by William Johnstone and, in the present, by Paolozzi and Ian Hamilton Finlay. In Geddes's own time, it was the ideals that they shared with him which inspired such remarkable images as Henry and Hornel's collaborative painting of the *Druids* (1890) and in Paris at the height of the Modernist revolution one of the few paintings by any artist to attempt to focus on a grand scale some kind of social idealism was Fergusson's *Les Eus* (c. 1911). It is a picture which takes up the theme of Matisse's *La Danse* perhaps, but which also looks back to the image of the dance of David Allan or Wilkie as epitomising, not simple hedonism, but social harmony under nature. As an image of dance, it was echoed too by William Johnstone in his painting *Point in Time* (1929–33), a picture which in its inspiration paralleled MacDiarmid, but which in its realisation was closer to Neil Gunn's search for the metaphysical extension of self in the presence of collective memory in the landscape – a metaphysical society extended in time as much as space and a vision which perhaps also underlies the brilliant paintings of Iona done by Cadell and Peploe.

Johnstone's picture epitomises the ideals of the Scots Renaissance and the investment of the Scottish identity in this history. As such it is perhaps as close as one can come to the present in attempting to outline a canon. It is important though that the interchange between the arts that characterised that movement as it had characterised Scottish culture so often before has also been a source of strength for contemporary Scottish artists. Is Ian Hamilton Finlay, for instance, artist or poet? Whichever he is, his garden, if it can be made secure for the future, will surely be one of the canonical achievements of Scottish art.

So how does this Scottish achievement fit into the wider European canon and what effect does its incorporation have on the conventional account of that structure? This conventional canon has a very long pedigree. Its chronological base reflects its origins in Pliny who gives an account of the art of classical Greece and, in so doing, incorporates into it the idea of evolution, of progression measured in terms of skill and leading to a high or classical state from which also there is a decline. In literature this could not be so simple as the universal model was Homer, whose place was at the beginning of its evolution. Thus from the start, the canon in art incorporated a progressive, historical structure in a way that the canon in literature has never done. Indeed, still today in universities, there are departments of literature 'tout court', but of art *history*. Vasari adapted and redefined this structure for the modern world. His *Vite* is a brilliant chronicle, but, adapting Pliny's model, it is structured on the idea of a progressive achievement, leading up to a climax in the High Renaissance and in Vasari's own time, the art of Michelangelo. Thus, also like Pliny, Vasari combined a qualitative canon with a progressive one.

A progressive canon means that as it defines the best, it also reveals how each generation builds upon the achievement of the one before. It shows how these 'best' elements hang together in a chain to form a greater unity. As it is a chain, a proven contribution to the structure as a whole, the status of link, is a necessary qualification for inclusion. In other words, there is an important relative dimension to the canon. It is not just the absolute achievement of an artist (or school) that counts. It is also the extent to which it focusses what is deemed essential in what has gone before, then transmutes and transmits it to what comes after. This is important because it means that by definition this canon is exclusive on grounds that have nothing to do with any absolute idea of quality.

Vasari's vision is also exclusive in the way that it is shaped geographically and from him we have inherited the belief that the true tradition belongs in one place. Following Vasari, our own idea of the progress of western art is based on the art of Italy. The art of northern Europe has largely been excluded from a place at the heart of the canon though of course, individually, such artists as Rembrandt and Vermeer have unquestioned canonical status.

Among scholars, there have of course been many honourable exceptions to this particular kind of myopia. To name just a few, Kenneth Clarke's *Rembrandt and the Italian Renaissance*[7] is a classic study of the irrelevance of such scholars' lines of demarcation to the vitality of the artistic imagination. Robert Rosenblum's *Modern Painting and the Northern Romantic Tradition*, written twenty years ago,[8] on the other hand makes a good case for the distinctiveness of the northern tradition and its contribution to the creation of canonical modernism, but even in that book his attitude to French art suggests at times that the author feels he is being audaciously unorthodox to suggest that the modern tradition is not monolithic (and French). More recently, Svetlana Alpers in *The Art of Describing*[9] made the first really serious attempt to analyse the intellectual and imaginative basis of Dutch art which, excepting Rembrandt and Vermeer as we have seen, has never been comfortably incorporated into the canon. Dutch art is empirical and the canon, by definition an academic idea, is dominated by idealism. Alpers's undertaking ought to have altered this perspective by showing how empiricism is at the heart of western art, but it does not do so because implicitly she accepts that Dutch art *is* apart, that its objectives *are* different and so her brilliant illumination of it does not alter our understanding of all the rest.

This bias also immediately affects Scottish art, for it is integrally part of the Northern tradition and specifically of the tradition that draws on the double helix of the Reformation and empiricism. This certainly shaped Scottish art, but also, much more than has been recognised, the whole evolution of progressive art in Europe within which, therefore, Scottish art may be integral rather than peripheral.

It was Horace Walpole writing in the 1760s who set the standard for British art writing. Implicitly he endorsed the canonical position, by presenting the history of art in Britain as a self-contained chronicle, and to meet any accusations of misplaced pride in a non-canonical tradition he used the unassuming title *Anecdotes of the Painters*. The first accounts of art in Scotland followed this model. Robert Brydall did so with great scholarship in his *History of Art in Scotland*.[10] It was James Caw who was the formative writer on Scottish art, however. In *Scottish Painting 1620–1908* he chose a Vasarian model and sought to present a progression in order to define a specific characteristic for art in Scotland – a Scottish canon in fact. He defined it thus:

> That a small country like Scotland should have produced so much art in little more than a century is notable, but that so large a proportion should be of excellent quality is indeed wonderful. Caring more for the signifi-cance and beauty of common things than for the far-off or fanciful, it possesses at its best a keen and dramatic perception of character and situation, a profound love of Nature, and a touch of poetic glamour expressed with an instinct for the essentials of impression, whether realism or decoration be in the ascendant, a dexterous and masculine quality of handling, combined with a fine use of paint, and a use of colour which assures it a distinct and honourable place.[11]

These things were fulfilled in his view in the work of his contemporaries. Writing more than sixty years later, however, the next significant contributors to the history of Scottish art, the Irwins, eschewed any such value judgment, or even the proposition that there might be Scottish canon, and so they called their book *Scottish Painters at Home and Abroad*.[12]

Caw's definition of the basic characteristics of the Scottish canon is instructive. Although the chronological limits of his book stretch back to 1620, in this passage he speaks only of the painting of the preceding century. His account is nevertheless almost entirely concerned with the empirical in painting, the observation of common things and the physical qualities of painting itself. He specifically excludes the metaphysical, the 'far-off or fanciful' as he calls it, and he hardly explores the possibility of shared experience between artists in different media. Caw's views were enduring and indeed my own view still coincides with his to an important degree in its essentials, except for the last part; the 'masculine quality of handling, combined with a fine use of paint, and . . . of colour.' Here I would part company with him, though the autonomy of paint was still an unchallenged creed for artists like Robin Philipson, while the role of colour and handling can still be put forward as a respectable definition of the characteristics of the 'Scottish school'.

In spite of Caw, however, on its own Scottish art would be ethnography, but to see it as part of a European tree, as Baldinucci described the history of art,[13] even though the Scottish contribution to European art is quantitatively a small one, involves changing our perspective of the whole. This is not just hyperbole and it is not because of the achievement of the painters alone, but because of the key place of Scottish thought, of which the painters were part, in a Europe dominated, as I suggested above, by the double helix of the Reformation tradition and empiricism; ideas and phenomena which have been excluded from the conventional view of the European canon by virtue of its origins.

Scotland is an integral part of northern Europe. In the days of sea communication this was not so difficult to recognise, for setting out from Scotland the nearest destinations were in the Netherlands, Denmark, Norway and the Baltic (also later Canada.) Southern England was just as far away as most of these. It was only with the development of land transport that England came to stand between Scotland and the Continent. Even though that was so, art history raises another barrier. It is incorrigibly centred on the achievement of the old classical world, but in fact by the late sixteenth century the North Sea had become the cultural centre of gravity of Europe. In the struggles of the Reformation, the tension between this new centre and the old classical world became a self-conscious division of Europe into two rival blocks, one progressive, the other reactionary, and their rivalry was focussed in radically opposed aesthetic ideas.

That in the North this was consciously identified with empirical thought and its opposition to idealism was demonstrated by Rembrandt on several occasions. For instance, he painted for Constantin Huyghens a picture of the *Blinding of Sampson* that clearly refers to the metaphorical blinding of Galileo and so explicitly opposed the freedom of empirical thought to pursue truth to the tyranny of belief imposed by authority and demanding obedience, not to the revelations of experience, but to its own arbitrary rulings. Thirty years later, in his painting of *The Oath of the Batavians* Rembrandt celebrated the rebellion of the Batavians, the proto-Dutch, against the Romans, a prototype for the successful struggle of the Northern Netherlands against the Spanish. In his picture, he deliberately cast the hero of the rebellion as grotesquely one-eyed. In so doing he challenged the authority of the idealist, classical tradition personified by Pliny. Pliny described how Apelles painted the one-eyed King Antigonous in a way that concealed his injury. Thus he displayed decorum by stressing, not the empirical reality of the individual, but the ideal. David Scougall echoed this in his painting of the squinting Marquis of Argyll and, in turn, Robert Fergusson focussed the same anti-Roman, anti-baroque sentiment as Rembrandt in 'On the Death of Scots Music':

> O Scotland! that could yence afford
> To bang the pith of Roman sword,
> Winna your sons, wi' joint accord,
>   To battle speed?
> And fight till Music be restor'd,
>   Which now lies dead.

To put the Dutch and Flemish painters back into the equation and to link the Scots directly to them introduces at the beginning of the modern era two key ideas, the empirical and the social. At the very beginning of the era thus defined, in such a painting as Breughel's *The Blind Leading the Blind*, we see sight as a metaphor for understanding. It is moral understanding, but the eye and so the artist is its witness. The Baconian basis of Dutch art is not a limitation therefore. It is an extension of the idea of art as knowledge when knowledge is truth and truth is moral power. From Breughel onwards, Netherlandish art is specifically social and in Breughel, just as in Wilkie, one can recognise the function of the artist defined in these terms.

The links between Scotland and the Netherlands are close, but they are also tantalising. In architecture they are clear, but elsewhere, although they are so close, they do not seem to be specific. It is an area that urgently needs study. Also, though there are apparent connections for the painters, they are not easily identified at a more theoretical level, while for the philosophers, it seems that the indirect connection through Locke and Shaftesbury was the most important, but it was in Scotland that their ideas were taken forward most dramatically by thinkers whose basic convictions were that experience is the basis of all knowledge and that what makes valuable and gives meaning to inquiry into the nature of experience is its social application. This had a direct reflection or parallel in painting as we have seen and if Hume's study was human nature so was that of Ramsay, whose methods were like his, empirical, but like his, too, it was empiricism tempered by imagination.

In painting, this is linked first with its Dutch antecedents and then also importantly with the anti-academic tradition in England. The leading figure here is Hogarth, whose own attitude to the canon was very interesting. He saw it as hostile to the modern art that he espoused, and manifested in the taste of the connoisseurs and the moves to establishing an Academy, against both of which his antagonism was aroused. As a consequence, Hogarth was consistently belittled by Reynolds, who became the spokesman for the conservative position, and such was the strength of this reaction that progressive artists like Blake and Barry were forced into opposition. Nothing like this happened to the Scots. Hogarth and Ramsay were friends and Hogarth's influence was important for Hamilton, Allan and Wilkie, though, working in the South, Wilkie clearly felt this pressure. It was only by a dual allegiance that he was able to preserve the progressive Scottish core of his art.

These relationships were not confined to the British Isles, however. After 1815, the Scots were of central importance in the new departures in French painting that are widely recognised as the opening moves in the story of modern art. In the painting of Gericault, Delacroix and Bonington there is clear evidence of a complex set of influences from Scotland through Scott and Wilkie, but also through Charles Bell and above all Thomas Reid, whose version of the empirical theory of perception based on intuition seems to have had a far-reaching influence on French nineteenth-century art.[14] Of course all this was not without precedent. The relationship between Chardin and Diderot and Diderot's own relationship to Shaftesbury all reflect the way in which the grounds for a similar approach to painting were available in France in the eighteenth century and, too, how it was linked with radical social ideas, but in the nineteenth century, as this gradually became the dominant ethos in France, the evidence for the part played by the Scots is clear. It is not surprising therefore that just as David's *Oath of the Horatii* owes a debt to Hamilton's *Death of Lucretia*, one of the French pictures universally accepted as standing at the head of the canon of modern painting, Courbet's *Apres Midi à Ornans*, appears to owe an explicit debt to Wilkie's *The Cotter's Saturday Night*, the central work in the Scottish canon.

If the key work in the Scottish canon can be integrated into the accepted European canon in this way without doing injury to its chain structure, it means that it may be possible to look in that canon for a reflection of the ideas that were central to the Scots achievement. If, only for the sake of argument, we were to put the ambitions of Scottish painters as near the centre of the European achievement and not the periphery, the result is quite interesting. We find that the ambition to describe the world in terms of the individual's experience becomes a central ambition. We find there is no metaphysical given, but that the metaphysical dimension must somehow be deduced from the empirical experience of the world and that, in this process, the imagination is the vital agent that allows the mind to reach beyond itself and first of all into the social dimension. With these as the central ambitions, we can construct a four-centuries project for modern art that provides a radical alternative to the clumsy, conventional canon with its archaic baggage of academic thought.

Already at the beginning of this period, in such great paintings as Breughel's *Carrying of the Cross*, the artist's viewpoint is that of a witness, a spectator who may not even be aware that the drama is happening. The generalisations of history and the ideal are incompatible with the particularities of individual, empirical experience. Nearly three hundred years later, in a specific commentary on Scott, Stendhal exploited just this viewpoint when, in *La Chartreuse de Parme*, he makes Fabrice ride through the battle of Waterloo without ever being quite sure that it has happened.

More than a century before Breughel, too, Van Eyck's extraordinary self-portrait (*Man in a Turban*) is utterly modern in a way that summarises some of the central concerns of modern art thus defined, the nature of experience and the tension between the physical and the metaphysical that is inherent in even the most tangible manifestations of one's own existence. On the picture, too, Van Eyck inscribed the legend 'Als Ich Kan', easily enough translated into Scots – 'All (that) I ken' – and so he proposed the basic question of the relationship between seeing and knowing that has shaped modern art. Fifty years later and in a Scottish context, in the Trinity College altarpiece, Hugo van der Goes likewise presented a profound reflection on the nature of knowledge. The donor, Edward Bonkil, an inhabitant of a world governed by the same rules as the world we live in, contemplates in a vision of the Trinity a metaphysical world in which a different reality prevails.[15] Such an image surely anticipates some of the central concerns of the Reformation and provides a preface to the argument that this alternative canon runs from the Reformation, through Breughel, Rembrandt and the Dutch, through the Scots and radical English and then to the nineteenth-century French and Impressionism, the high point of empirical painting. Throughout, its centre is located in the general region of that elusive point where the vectors of perceived truth and moral truth meet and whose coordinates Hume calculated more closely than most. But if, too, the artificial barrier that separates modern art from the older canon is removed, then modernism itself can be seen as part of this longer project. The idea of an artist whose art is truly anti-social, or even asocial, though it is a common enough modern phenomenon, is the travesty that is left if the imagination's social limbs are amputated. Its social role as it was identified by artists like Ramsay, Raeburn or Wilkie is still a vital part of the work of some of the greatest modern artists like Miro, Leger or Malevich, and in our own time, Paolozzi and Finlay. ❧

Talbot Rice Gallery, University of Edinburgh

1 *Scottish Art Since 1900*, National Galleries of Scotland, 1989.

2 See Duncan Macmillan, *Painting in Scotland: the Golden Age* (Oxford 1986) Chap.3, *passim*.

3 I have discussed this question and also Hamilton's relationship to Adam Smith in a forthcoming essay 'Woman as Hero; Gavin Hamilton's Radical Alternative'. It will be published by Manchester University Press late in 1993 in a collection ed. by Gill Perry, *Constructions of Masculinity and Feminity in Eighteenth Century Art*.

4 See note 3.

5 See Duncan Macmillan 'Truly National Designs: Alexander Runciman at Penicuik', *Art History* I, 1978.

6 Burns to Thomson, April 1796.

7 Kenneth Clarke, *Rembrandt and the Italian Renaissance* (London 1966).

8 Robert Rosenblum, *Modern Painting and the Northern Romantic Tradition* (London 1975).

9 Svetlana Alpers, *The Art of Describing* (Chicago 1983).

10 Robert Brydall, *History of Art in Scotland* (Edinburgh 1889).

11 James Caw, *Scottish Painting, Past and Present, 1620–1908* (Edinburgh 1908) p495.

12 David and Francina Irwin, *Scottish Painters at Home and Abroad 1700–1900* (London 1975).

13 Fillipo Baldinucci, 'L'Autore a che Legge', *Notizie de' Professori del Disegno etc* (1681).

14 I have discussed these relationships variously in 'Sources of French Narrative Painting; Between Three Cultures', *Apollo*, May 1993, in 'French Art and Scotch Philosophy', *Essays in Honour of Basil Skinner*, ed. Murdo MacDonald (Edinburgh 1993) and in 'Peinture, Philosphie et Psychiatrie: Gericault, Charles Bell et la Philosophie du Sens Commun', forthcoming papers of *Colloque Gericault* held at the Musée du Louvre, 1991.

15 See Duncan Macmillan, *Scottish Art 1460–1990* (Edinburgh 1990) p19–20.

ALASDAIR GRAY

Money

Between social unequals honesty is difficult and friendship impossible. Only snobs, perverts and the utterly desperate want intimacies with people much richer or poorer. Maybe in Iceland or Holland factory-owners and labourers relax by eating in each other's homes and going holidays together. If so they must have equally good houses, food, clothes and schools for their children— something like equality of income. The thing is impossible in Scotland or England. Mackay disagrees. He says the Scots have a tradition which lets them forget social differences. He says his father was gardener on a huge estate in the north and the owner was his dad's best friend. On very rainy days they sat in the gardener's shed and drank a bottle of whisky together. But equality of income, real or apparent, allows steadier friendship than equality of intoxication. I did not want to borrow money from Mackay because it proved I was poorer than him. He insisted on lending, which eventually ruined me.

To complete a profitable piece of business quickly I needed a thousand pounds cash and phoned to arrange a loan. My bank said I could have it at once at an interest of eleven per cent plus a forty-pound arrangement fee. I explained that I would repay in five days and was told that if I borrowed a thousand now I must repay one thousand one hundred and fifty, even if I repaid tomorrow. I groaned, said I would see them in half an hour, put down the phone and noticed Mackay was in the room. He had strolled in from his office next door. We did the same sort of work but were not competitors. When I got more business than I could handle I passed it to him, and vice versa.

He said, 'What have you to groan about?'

I told him and added, 'I can easily pay eleven per cent et cetera but I hate it. I belong to the financial past—all interest above five per cent strikes me as extortion.'

'I'll give you a thousand, interest free,' said Mackay pulling out his cheque book. While I explained why I never borrow money from friends he filled in a cheque, tore it off and held it out saying, 'Stop raving about equality and take this to my bank. I'll phone and they'll cash it at once. We're still equals—in an emergency you would do the same for me.'

I blushed because he was almost certainly wrong. Then I shrugged, took the cheque and said, 'If this is what you want, Mackay, all right. Fine. I'll return it within the week, or within a fortnight at most.'

'Harry, I know that. Don't worry,' said Mackay soothingly and started talking about something else. I felt grateful but angry because I hate feeling grateful. I also hated his easy assumption that his money was perfectly safe. Had I lent *him* a thousand pounds I would have worried myself sick until I got it back. If being aristocratic means preferring good manners to money then Mackay was acting like my superior. Did he think his dad's boozing sessions with Lord Glenbannock had *ennobled* the Mackays? The loan was already undermining our friendship.

Five days later my business was triumphantly concluded and I added a cheque for over ten thousand pounds to my bank account. I was strongly tempted *not* to repay Mackay at once, just to show him I was something more than decent, honest, dependable old Harry, but I stayed honest longer by remembering that if I repaid promptly I might borrow from him again. Handing him a cheque would have been as embarrassing as taking one so I decided to pay cash straight back into his bank account. Despite computerization my bank would have taken two or three days to transfer the money, which would have shifted repayment to the following week, so I collected ten crisp new hundred-pound notes in a smooth envelope, placed envelope in inner jacket pocket and walked the half mile toward Mackay's bank. The morning air was mild but fresh, the sky one sheet of high grey cloud which threatened rain but might hold off till nightfall.

Mackay's bank is at the end of a road where I lived when I was married and I seldom go there now. The buildings on one side have been erased and the foundations scooped out to make a cutting holding a six-lane motorway. Tenements and shops on the remaining side no longer have a thriving look. I was walking carefully along the cracked and pitted pavement when I heard a woman say, 'Harry, what are *you* doing here?'

She was thin, sprightly, short-haired and (like most attractive women nowadays) struck me as any age between sixteen and forty. I said I was going to a bank to repay money I owed. She looked like someone I knew so I said, 'How are your folk up at Ardnamurchan, Liz?'

She laughed and said, 'I'm *Mish*, you idiot! Come inside—Wee Dougie and Davenport and Roy and Roberta are there and we haven't seen you for ages.' I remembered none of these names but never say no to women who want me. It does not often happen. I followed her into The Whangie, though it was not a pub I liked. The best pubs had all been on the demolished side of the street.

The Whangie's customers may not have been prone to violence but I suspected they were, so the pleasure I felt at the sight of the drab brown dusty interior was wholly unexpected. It was exactly as it had been twenty or thirty years before, exactly like most Scottish pubs before the big breweries used extravagant tax reliefs to buy and remake them like Old English taverns or Spanish bistros. This was still a dour Scottish drinking-den which kept the prices down by spending nothing on appearances. The only wall decorations were solidly framed mirrors frosted with the names and emblems of defunct whisky blends. And the place was nearly empty, for it was soon after opening-time. Crying, 'Look who's here!' Mish led me to some people round a corner table, one of whom I recognized.

'Let me get you a drink, Harry,' he said, starting to stand, but, 'No no no sit down sit down' I said, hurrying to the bar. Outside the envelope in my inner jacket pocket I had just enough cash to buy a half pint of lager. I carried this back to the people in the corner. They made room for me.

A fashion note. None of us looked smart. The others wore jeans with shapeless denim or leather jackets, I wore my old tweed jacket and crumpled corduroys. Only my age marked me off from the rest, I thought, and not much. The only man I knew, a musician called Roy, was almost my age. The one oddity among us was the not-Mish woman, Roberta. Her hair was the colour of dry straw and stood straight upright on top of her skull, being clipped or shaved to thin stubble at the back and sides. The wing of her right nostril was pierced by several fine little silver rings, her lipstick was dull purple. She affected me like someone with a facial deformity so to avoid staring hard I ignored her completely. This was easy as she never said a word the whole time I was in The Whangie. She seemed depressed about something: when the others spoke to her she answered by sighing or grunting or shrugging her shoulders.

First they asked how I was getting on and I answered, 'Not bad—not good.' The truth was that like many professional folk nowadays I am doing extremely well, even though I have to borrow money sometimes, but it would have been unkind to say how much better off I was than them. I did not ask how they were getting on as they were obviously unemployed. Why else did they drink, and drink very slowly, at half past eleven on Thursday morning? I avoided distressing topics by talking to Roy, the musician. We had met at a party where he sang and played the fiddle really well. Since then I had seen him busking in the shopping precincts, and had passed quickly on the opposite side of the street to avoid embarrassing him, for he was too good a musician to be living that way. I asked him about the people who had held the party, not having seen them since. Neither had Roy so we discussed the party. Ten minutes later we had nothing more to say about it and I had drunk my half pint. I stood up and said, 'Have to go now folks.'

They fell silent and looked at me. I sensed, maybe mistakenly, that they expected something, and blushed, and spoke carefully to avoid stammering: 'You see, I would like to buy a round before I go but I've no cash on me. I mean, I've plenty of money in my bank—and I have my cheque book here— could one of you cash a cheque for five pounds?—I promise it won't stott.'

Nobody answered. I realized none of them had five pounds, or the means of turning my cheque into cash if they had.

'Cash it at the bar, Harry,' suggested Mish.

'I would like to—but do you think the barman will do it without a cheque card?'

'No cheque card?' said Mish on a shrill note.

'None! I've never had a cheque card. If I had I would lose it. I'm always losing things. But the barmen in Tennent's cash my cheques without one . . .'

'Jimmy!' cried Davenport, who had a black beard and a firm manner and had waved to the barman, 'Jimmy, this pal of ours wants to cash a cheque. He's Harry Haines, a well-known character in the west end with a good going business—'

'In fact he's loaded,' said Mish—

'—and you would oblige us by cashing a cheque for him. He's left his cheque card at home.'

'Sorry,' said the barman, 'there's nothing I can do about that,' and he turned his back on us.

'I'm sorry too,' I told them helplessly.

'You,' Mish told me, 'are a mean old fart. You are not only mean, you are totally uninteresting.'

At these words my embarrassment vanished and I cheered up. I no longer minded being superior. With an air of mock sadness I said, 'True! So I must leave you. Goodbye folks.'

I think the three men were also amused by the turn things had taken. They said cheerio to me quite pleasantly.

I left The Whangie and went toward Mackay's bank, carefully remembering the previous twelve minutes to see if I might have done better with them. I did not regret entering The Whangie with Mish. She had pleasantly excited me and I had not known she only saw me as a source of free drink. True, I had talked boringly—had bored myself as well as them—but interesting topics would have emphasized the social gulf between us. I might have amused them with queer stories about celebrities whose private lives are more open to me than to popular journalism (that was probably how the duke entertained Mackay's father between drams in the tool shed) but it strikes me as an unpleasant way to cadge favour with unequals. I was pleased to think I had been no worse then a ten-minute bore. I had made a fool of myself by appearing to want credit for a round of drinks I could not buy, but that kind of foolery hurts nobody. If Mish and her pals despised me for it good luck to them. I did not despise myself for it, or only slightly. In the unexpected circumstances I was sure I could not have behaved better.

The idea of taking a hundred-pound note from Mackay's money and buying a round of drinks only came to me later. So did the idea of handing the note to Mish, saying 'Share this with the others,' and leaving fast before she could reply. So did the best idea of all: I could have laid five hundred-pound notes on the table, said 'Conscience money, a hundred each,' and hurried off to put the rest in Mackay's account. Later I could have told him, 'I paid back half what I owe today, but you'll have to wait till next week for the rest. I've done something stupid with it.' As he heard the details his mouth would open wider and wider or his frown grow sterner and sterner. At last he would say, 'That's the last interest-free loan you get from me'—or something else. But he would have been as astonished as the five in the pub. I would have proved I was not predictable. Behaving like that would have changed my character for the better. But I could not imagine doing such things then. I can only imagine them since I changed for the worse.

I left The Whangie and went toward Mackay's bank, brooding on my recent adventure. No doubt there was a smug little smile on my lips. Then I noticed someone was walking beside me and heard a low voice say, 'Wait a minute.' I stopped. My companion was Roberta, who stood staring at me. She was breathing hard, perhaps with the effort of overtaking me, and her mouth was set in something like a sneer. I could not help looking straight at her now. Everything I saw—weird hair and sneering face, shapeless leather jacket with hands thrust into flaps below her breasts, baggy grey jeans turned up at the bottoms to show clumsy thick-soled boots laced high up the ankles—all this insulted my notion of what was attractive. But her alert stillness as the breathing calmed made me feel very strange, as if I had seen her years ago, and often. To break the strangeness I said sharply, 'Well?'
Awkwardly and huskily she said, 'I don't think you're mean or uninteresting. I like older men.'
Her eyes were so wide open that I saw the whole circle of the pupils, one brown, one blue. There was a kind of buzzing in my blood and the nearby traffic sounded fainter. I felt stronger and more alive than I had felt for years—alive in a way I had never expected to feel again after my marriage went wrong. Her sneer was now less definite, perhaps because I felt it on my own lips. Yes, I was leering at her like a gangster confronting his moll in a 1940 cinema poster and she was staring back as if terrified to look anywhere else. I was fascinated by the thin stubble at the sides of her head above the ears. It must feel exactly like my chin before I shaved in the morning. I wanted to rub it hard with the palms of my hands. I heard myself say, 'You want money I suppose. How?'

She murmured that I could visit my bank before we went to her place—or afterward, if I preferred. My leer became a wide grin. I patted my inner pocket and said, 'No need for a bank, honey. I got everything you want right here. And we'll take a taxi to my place, not yours.'

I spoke with an American accent, and the day turned into one of the worst in my life. 🐝

Museum

The following report on my reading was made near the end of my 16th year in 1951, and retained by my English teacher, Mr Meikle, whose widow gave it to me after his death in the spring of 1993. It was written with a steel-ribbed pen dipped into a squat glass bottle (if I wrote at home) or (if I wrote at school) into an inkwell — a truncated cone of glazed white earthenware less than two inches high, whose wide end was closed by a glazed white earthenware disc slightly more than an inch in diameter, a disc with a hole in the centre to admit the knib and a projecting lip all round which let it hang snugly in the circular hole cut for it in our desk tops. In 1951 ball point pens had been commercially marketed for several years, but most British schools forbad their use because it would reduce the quality of our handwriting. In those days most employers still preferred clerks whose penwork was clear and elegant, so schools encouraged it. In 1951 my writing, like nowadays, was very clear but not at all elegant, having changed little since I learned to draw words when four or five. The letters are distinctly shaped and connected, but the loops of a, d, g and q are almost circular, the loop of e a wide oval, as are the ascending and descending loops of b, f, g, h, j, k and l. All ascenders and descenders are short. I could never slope the vertical strokes slightly to the right as we were urged, so my vertical strokes are exactly so, or incline as much to the left as the right. I am almost certain this form was copied out at home from an earlier, messier attempt because I am prone to afterthoughts ████████████, and ██ some spaces for titles have been neatly filled up without a single blot or correction.

WHITEHILL SENIOR SECONDARY SCHOOL

Report on Reading

Name of Pupil *Alasdair Gray.*   Class in Sept. _____

Scott *None*

Kipling *Just So Stories.*
The Jungle Books (1 and 2)
Seven Seas.
Stalky and Co.
Puck of Pook's Hill.

Dickens *The Christmas Books.*
Barnaby Rudge.
Little Dorrit.
Oliver Twist.
David Copperfield.
Pickwick Papers.

Trollope *None.*

Conan Doyle *The Sign of Four.*
A Study in Scarlet.
The Lost World.
Casebook of Sherlock Holmes.
The Poison Belt.
The Speckled Band.

Bennett *The Card.*

Thackeray *The Rose and the Ring.*

Shaw *Man + Superman. Back to Methuselah. The Devil's Disciple. Widower's Houses. Mrs Warren's Profession. The Apple Cart. The Showing up of Blanco Posnett. St Joan. John Bull's other Island. Pygmalion. Candida. Arms and the Man. Androcles, Captain Brassbound's Conversion. Misalliance. The Doctor's Dilemma. Major Barbara. Heartbreak House. O'Flaherty V.C. The Philanderer. The Man of Destiny. You Never can Tell. A Village Wooing. Press Cuttings. The Glimpse of Reality. On the Rocks. The Black Girl in Search of God. Scraps and Shavings. Intelligent Woman's Guide to Capitalism, Socialism, Sovietism and Fascism.*

Charlotte Bronte

Jane Eyr.

Wodehouse *None.*

Conrad *Youth.*
Gaspar Ruiz.
The Shadow Line.
Under Western Eyes.
Chance.
Last Essays.

Emily Bronte.
Wuthering Heights.

over/

Galsworthy *None.* Jack London *None*

Barrie *None.* Buchan *The Thirty nine Steps.*
Prester John.
Greenmantle.
The Powerhouse.

R.L. Stevenson *Treasure Island.* Siegfried Sassoon *none.*
Kidnapped.
Dr. Jeykhill and Mr. Hyde.
The Master of Ballantrae,
a childs Garden of Verse.
Virginibus puerisque.
Several Short Stories

H.G. Wells *The Time machine.* Hugh Walpole *Mr. Perrin and Mr. Trail.*
all the Short Stories. *Jeremy.*
The Invisible man.
The Food of the Gods.
The King who was King
The First men on the moon.
the Island of Dr Moreau. The History of
Mr. Polly. Tono Bungay. The Shape of
things to come. a Study of History.
The War of the Worlds. An Experiment in
autobiography.
Chesterton Neil Munro *The Daft Days.*
The Napoleon of Notting Hill
The Innocence of Father Brown
The Coloured Lands (essays, short stories)

H.V. Morton *None.* Jane Austen *None.*

Hardy *None.* Meredith *The Ordeal of Richard Feverel.*

George Borrow *Lavengro.* *Candide (By voltaic), Turgenev's "on the Eve."*
Romany Rye. Other authors and titles *Tristram Shandy.*
Sentimental Journey, Robinson Crusoe.
History of Jonathon Wilde the great, Les Miserables.
The Hunchback of Notre Dame. Gulliver's Travels.
Cranford, Erewhon + Erewhon Revisited.
Tales of mystery + Imagination, Twenty-
Thousand Leagues Under the Sea. Alice in
Wonderland + Through the Lookingglass. The Water
-Babies. (by Kingsley, Unabridged) Ape and Essence.
The Brave New World (Aldous Huxley), 1984, and
Animal Farm (George Orwell), Life of Samuel
Johnson (Boswell). The Golden ass (Unabridged -
Apuleius). Home of Mankind, Story of Mankind,
Arts of Mankind, Liberation of Mankind. Lives,
(by Hendrick VanLoon). The Complete Works of
Edward Lear. Peer Gynt, The Wild Duck, an Enemy
of The People — (Henrick Ibsen). Goethes Faust (Part I)

JCW/MB/16.8.50

The above list is not ~~entirely~~ truthful. I had read only a little beyond the start of <u>Barnaby Rudge</u> and Conrads <u>Under Western Eyes</u>, abandoning the first because I am impatient of man-made mysteries and Dickens 18th ~~century~~ century seemed less interestingly furnished than his 19th; abandoning the second because I hated stories about lives ruined by treachery. I had read nothing by Arnold Bennet but had heard a radio talk about ~~The Card~~ <u>The Card</u> with some dramatized excerpts, and knew I could answer questions on it. I had not read <u>The Intelligent Womans Guide to Capitalism</u> etcetera because to this day I cannot thoroughly read a work of politics, sociology or philosophy which does not describe particular instances. I am now sure that Shaws treatise has many particular instances, but when sixteen the title made me doubt it. Nor had I done more than read the opening chapters of Wells <u>Study of History</u> in the abbreviated Pelican edition, but I wanted my teachers to think me a greater scholar than I was — a greater scholar than ~~they were~~.

Explaining how, and where, and when I came to read the other books would take at least a year, so I will comment on very few. The complete plays of Bernard Shaw and Henrik Ibsen stood on the middle shelf of a bookcase in my parents beside Carlyles <u>French Revolution</u>, Macauleys <u>Essays</u>, <u>The History of the Working Classes in Scotland</u> and <u>Our Noble Families</u> by Tom Johnson, a Thinkers Library volume called <u>Humanities Gain From Unbelief</u>, an anthology of extracts for atheists called <u>Lift Up Your Heads</u>, a large blue-grey bound volume with <u>The Miracle of Life</u> stamped in gold on the spine. This contained essays on The Dawn of Life, What ~~Evolution~~ Evolution Means, Life that has Vanished, Evolution as the Clock Ticks, The Animal Kingdom, The Plant Kingdom, Man's Family Tree, Races of Mankind, The Human Machine at Work, Psychology Through the Ages, Discoverers of Life's Secrets. The 476 pages (excluding the index) were ~~about~~ half ~~of them~~ given to black-and-white photographs and diagrams. The middle shelf also held Shaws <u>Quintescence of Ibsenism</u> and <u>The Adventures of the Black Girl in Search of God</u>, and I believe the last was the first adult narrative brought ~~in~~ to my attention, though I cannot remember it. I remember first reading it with pleasure and excitement in my middle teens, but years later   my father told me he had read it to me when I was wee — perhaps four years old. The story presents an evolutionary view of human faith through the quest of a black girl through the African bush. Converted to Christianity by an English missionary she sets out to find god, not doubting he can be found on earth, and ▓▓▓▓▓▓▓ encounters in various clearings the gods of Moses, Job and Isaiah, then meeting Ecclesiastes the Preacher, Jesus, Mahomet, the founders of the Christian sects, an expedition of scientific rationalists, Voltaire the sceptic and George Bernard Shaw the socialist, who teach her that god should not be searched for but worked for, by cultivating the small piece of world in our power as intelligently and unselfishly as possible.

The moral of this story is as high as human wisdom has reached, but I cannot have grasped it then. My father told me that I kept asking, "Will the next god be the real one Daddy?" No doubt I would have liked the black girl to have at last met a universal maker like my father: vaster, of course, but with an equally vital sense of my importance. I am glad he did not teach me to believe in that, for I would have had to unlearn it. But my first encounter with this book was in a pre-history I have forgotten or suppressed, though I returned to it later. It was a beautifully made book with crisp clear black-woodcuts decorating ▓▓▓ covers, title page and text in a style reminiscent of Eric Gill. Like the text it convincingly blended the mundane and   exotic.

This was all on the middle shelf of the bedroom bookcase. The shelf above was blocked by the orange-red spines of ▓ Left Wing book club, four fifths of it being the collected works of Lenin in English: dense text with no pictures or conversations in it at all. The bottom shelf was exactly filled by the Harmsworth Encyclopaedia, because the bookcase had sold along with the Encyclopaedia by the publisher, who owned the Daily Record in which they were first advertised. This contained many pictures, mostly grey monochrome photographs, but each alphabetical section had a complex line drawing in front, a crowded landscape in which an enthroned figure representing Ancient History (for example) was surrounded by orders of Architecture, an Astronomical telescope, glimpses of Australia and the Arctic with Amundson, and an Armadillo and Aardvark rooting around a discarded Anchor. ~~~~~~~~~ I gathered that these volumes contained explanations of everything there is and had been, with lives of everyone important. ~~~~~ The six syllables of the name EN—CY—CLO—PAED—I—A seemed to sum up these ~~~~~~~ thick brown books which summed up the universe, so saying it gave me a sense of power ~~~~ confirmed by the pleasure this gave my parents. But the four colour plates ~~~~~~~~~~~~ showing flags of all nations and heraldic coats-of-arms ~~~~~~~~~~~~~~~~~ gave ~~ an undiluted pleasure which was purely sensuous. ~~~~~~~~~~~~~~~~~~~ ~~~~~ I was fascinated by the crisp oblongs and lozenges ~~~~~~~~~ holding ~~~~~~~~~~~~ ~~~~~~~~~ Blues, reds yellows, greens, blacks and whites ~~~~~~~~~~~~~~ combining in patterns more vivid and easily seen than anywhere else, apart from our Christmas decorations. I got a similar but more complex pleasure from Wills cigarette picture cards, gathered for me by my father into slim little squareish pale grey albums of this costing a penny, when empty. There was an album for Garden Flowers, Garden Hints, British Wild Animals, Railway Equipment, Cycling and Aircraft of the Royal Airforce. These cards, ~~~~~ five to each page, were windows into places where ~~~ weather was always a bright afternoon and everything was in its best condition. Cigarette card albums, encyclopaedia and The Miracle of Life are still a source of information and imagery for me, though I have since added others. Together with The Black Girl in Search of God they occupied the place an illustrated family bible may have held in the ~~~~~~ lives of my father's parents, who died ~~~~~~~~~~~ years before I was born.

From ~~~ my ~~~ four and a half years before the second world war began — or from the five years before it hotted up — I also remember a big book of Hans Anderson fairy tales, well illustrated, which must have been read to me because I cannot remember not knowing ~~~~ The Marsh Kings Daughter and The Brave Tin Soldier and The Tinderbox and The Little Match Girl and The Snow Queen and the Little Mermaid and their mingling of ~~~~~

magic with the ordinary urban and domestic, and their terrible sad sense of how quickly things ~~XXXX~~ change and are lost to faithful people whose affections do not change. There were ~~XXX~~ flower-fairy books, Rupert Bear annuals (also in ~~XXXX~~ sunny colours) ~~but Christopher~~ Milnes' House at Pooh Corner and two Christopher Robin verse books. All these books were left behind when we flitted from our home until the ~~XXXXX~~ war ended, ~~XXX~~ spending the last three or four years of it in   Wetherby, a Yorkshire market town.

And there I read with delight   Loftings Dr Doolittle books, Kiplings <u>Just So Stories</u>, Thackerays <u>The Rose and the Ring</u> (all illustrated by their authors), the <u>Alice</u> books, and Kingsleys <u>Waterbabies</u> in (as I was careful to mention in the 1951   school reading report) the <u>unabridged</u> version. Also <u>The Wind in the Willows</u>, though a chapter called <u>The Piper at the Gates of Dawn</u> embarrassed and annoyed me. I dislike ~~XXXXX~~ mysteriously superior presences. ~~XXXXXXX~~
~~XXXXX~~ ~~XXXXXXXX~~
With the exception of   <u>The Wind in the Willows</u> and Thackeray book ~~XXXX~~ all these had (like Shaws <u>Black Girl</u> fable) ~~XXXXX~~ an <u>encyclopaedic</u> scope, mingling humans,   animals and magic   , going under the earth and soaring over it, making as free with time and space as any Indian or African creation myth, or ~~XXXXX~~ <u>Paradise Lost</u>, or Goethes <u>Faust</u>, ~~X~~ or Ibsens <u>Peer Gynt</u>. And all these books were strengthened by the   artistic   union of the normally impossible. That the fairy-tale tyrant of Crim Tartary should   be a very commonplace Victorian pater familias.   at home — that, even so, when unexpectedly enchanted by a lovely chambermaid he instinctively propose   in Shakespearian rhyming couplets to marry her after drowning his first wife — seemed to me wonderfully comic, because though impossible it was appropriate.

Which brings my reading to the age of ten without even mentioning Kingsleys <u>Heroes</u>, Hawthornes <u>Tanglewood Tales</u>, a version of the <u>Odessay</u> for children and <u>Gods, Graves and Scholars</u>, a book about the archeological discovery of Troy, Mycenae, Minoa, Babylon, Nineveh, Egypt and Yucatan. Time to stop.

Notes on contributors

Colin Kidd is a Fellow of All Souls College, Oxford, and the author of *Subverting Scotland's Past* (Cambridge University Press, 1993). He will take up a lectureship in Scottish History at Glasgow University in September, 1994

Marshall Walker was born and educated in Scotland and has been Professor of English at the University of Waikato since 1981. He is currently President of the Scottish Studies Association there and working on a commissioned account of Scottish literature since 1707. He is an occasional broadcaster on literary and musical subjects for Radio New Zealand.

Donald MacAulay was born in the Isle of Lewis and educated at Stornoway, Aberdeen and Cambridge. He has taught in universities in Edinburgh, Dublin and Aberdeen and is now Professor of Celtic in the University of Glasgow. As well as his own verse he has published an anthology of modern Scottish Gaelic poems and articles on Gaelic literature, linguistics and sociolinguistics.

Robert Crawford is Lecturer in Modern Scottish Literature in the School of English at the University of St Andrews and an Associate Director of the St Andrews Scottish Studies Institute (SASSI). His collections of poetry include *A Scottish Assembly* (Chatto, 1990) and he is the author of *Devolving English Literature* (Clarendon Press, 1992). His latest book, *Identifying Poets*, was published by Edinburgh University Press in 1993.

David Hill Radcliffe is the author of *Forms of Reflection: Genre and Culture in Meditational Writing* (1993). He is working on a history of Spenser criticism and a catalogue of early imitations and commentary on Spenser. He teaches eighteenth-century British literature at Virginia Polytechnic Institute and State University.

John Purser is a Glasgow-based composer, broadcaster and writer. His books include *Scotland's Music* (Mainstream, 1992) and his plays include *Carver*, a full-length radio play about Scotland's greatest composer. He has composed opera and solo guitar works, as well as being responsible for the thirty-programme series for BBC Radio Scotland on the history of Scottish music.

Duncan Macmillan is a Reader in Fine Art and Curator of the Talbot Rice Gallery, University of Edinburgh. He is an Hon. Academician of the Royal Scottish Academy and a Fellow of the Royal Society of Arts. He has written books and articles on Scottish art from the eighteenth and nineteenth centuries, including *Painting in Scotland: the Golden Age, 1707–1843* (Phaidon, 1986) and *Scottish Art 1460–1990* (Mainstream, 1990). He is currently preparing a study of Scotland and France in the Enlightenment.

Alasdair Gray's fourth novel, *Poor Things*, was published in 1992. *Ten Tales Tall and True* appeared in 1993. He is currently working on a collection of literary prefaces. 🍎

Scotlands

*The Interdisciplinary Journal
of Scottish Culture*

◆

SPECIAL OFFER FOR NEW SUBSCRIBERS!
SEE BACK FOR DETAILS

Edinburgh University Press

Scotlands

The Interdisciplinary Journal of Scottish Culture

Edinburgh University Press are pleased to announce the launch of an exciting new journal, the first to be devoted to Scottish culture in all its forms. *Scotlands* seeks to be enlightening and comprehensive, featuring fresh academic work on a wide range of subjects.

In the last decade Scottish studies have grown and flourished. *Scotlands* will create a forum for the sharing of insight and enthusiasm, for debate and consensus. Each issue will contain essays from leading scholars in the arts, literature, music, history and current affairs. Individually, these articles will be essential reading for everyone interested in Scottish culture; collectively, they will construct the crucial debate on the state of Scotland today.

Published twice yearly by Edinburgh University Press

What's in Issues 1 & 2...?

Order Form

Return this form to:
Subscriptions
Edinburgh University Press Ltd
22 George Square
Edinburgh
EH8 9LF

| | Please enter my subscription to
Scotlands, Volume 1, 1994

| | I enclose the correct remittance
(please make cheques payable to
Edinburgh University Press Ltd)

| | Please debit my Visa/Mastercard
account number

_____

Expiry date ____ / ____

Name _____

Address _____

_____

_____

Postcode _____

Country _____

Signature _____

Date _____

Subscription Rates

Volume 1, 1994

ISSN 1350-7508

FIRST YEAR SPECIAL OFFER!

Take out a subscription to
Scotlands today and save 10%.

Normal subscription for a year - £20
Special subscription offer - £18

Simply return this form with
your year's remittance to EUP.
p&p free within the UK.

Scotlands is also available
from bookshops.

Issues will appear in
January & July

Institutions
UK and EEC	£32
Overseas	£35
N. America	$60

Individuals (Normal rate)
UK and EEC	£20
Overseas	£22
N. America	$38.50

Postage:
Surface postage is included in the
subscription. Please add £5 or $10
for airmail delivery.